To JERRY
SEMPER FI
Rom 13:4

Ephesians: God's Battle Plan for Spiritual Warfare

Ephesians: God's Battle Plan for Spiritual Warfare

A Combat Veteran's View

CWO-4 Ray R. Fairman USMCR (Ret.),PhD

United States Marine Corps (Retired) 1963–1996

Christian Soldier (Active Duty)

1962–Present

iUniverse, Inc.
New York Lincoln Shanghai

Ephesians: God's Battle Plan for Spiritual Warfare
A Combat Veteran's View

iUniverse books may be ordered through booksellers or by contacting:

iUniverse
2021 Pine Lake Road, Suite 100
Lincoln, NE 68512
www.iuniverse.com
1-800-Authors (1-800-288-4677)

"If you want to talk the talk, then you better train to walk the walk."

All Narrative and Instructional Scripture (unless otherwise indicated) taken from the NEW AMERICAN STANDARD BIBLE.

All Outline Scripture taken from the King James Version of the Bible.

ISBN-13: 978-0-595-36445-9 (pbk)
ISBN-13: 978-0-595-80877-9 (ebk)
ISBN-10: 0-595-36445-4 (pbk)
ISBN-10: 0-595-80877-8 (ebk)

Printed in the United States of America

Dedication

This work, however amateur my efforts may appear to some, is dedicated to the One who inspired me to write it and who helped me uncover many personal truths documented herein. Truths, which He intended for me not only to learn but to experience and teach as well. He has also blessed me during my lifelong march through Ephesians with the ability to uniquely express these experiences as both a combat-experienced Marine and as a law enforcement officer. As my daily knowledge of His teachings increases, I acquire an even greater understanding and a more distinct appreciation for them. It is from my experiences that I intend to help you understand the message Paul was trying to convey to the Ephesians.

The Lord knew (long before I did) how I needed to be prepared for the multitude of spiritual battles for which He has faithfully equipped me. I want to thank Him for being my God and for patiently and diligently shadowing me through my basic training, then mentoring me through additional advanced training. He knew I would eventually require this training, as the battles I faced became complex and my responsibilities diverse and demanding. Though God well knows I have lost many individual battles along the way, I have never feared losing the war, for He has equipped and trained me well. Christ alone won the most crucial battle ever fought centuries ago on Calvary's Cross: the battle for the salvation of mankind. Christians know the war is over, but just as in earthly conflict, lives are often lost. In these last days of spiritual warfare, many souls will also be lost before Our Lord returns in triumph.

Contents

Acknowledgments

As I begin this undertaking, I would like to recognize the patience and support of my wife, Joan, who has put up with my eccentric, sporadic, and often seemingly impractical concentration on this project. It must have seemed to her (like it often did to me) that I would never finish. Except for her enthusiasm and her willingness to act as a sounding board, its conclusion might have been in doubt. I would also like to recognize the influence of my son, Ryan, and his wife, Dayna, whose desire to serve God gave me the inspiration to complete this work. I also want to thank every Christian I have come in contact with during my lifelong learning crusade. God has endowed me with an ability to internalize, recall, and regurgitate lesson after lesson that I have learned throughout my life, though they may not be repeated exactly as I learned them. Should you be one who taught me a lesson, shared an exhortation, or provided a compassionate chastisement: thank you. You will, I hope, find the fruits of your refrain, prayer, or sermon intertwined somewhere in this effort.

Foreword

Why in the world would anyone embark on a journey without knowing where he or she would end up? I have no earthly idea. I can only assure you that they would. I have started down one of those less-traveled roads in my own life by deciding to write my thoughts on spiritual warfare, thoughts that I pray are not my thoughts at all but experiences the Holy Spirit wants me to document in this humble manuscript.

I have served in the armed forces of my country for more than thirty-three years, wearing several of its military uniforms (U.S. Marine Corps Active Duty and Reserve—twenty-seven years; U.S. Army Reserve—four years; and U.S. Air Force Reserve—two years). At the age of seventeen, I swore to support and defend the Constitution of the United States against all enemies, foreign or domestic, and to faithfully support and defend the ideals of my homeland.

I have also taken several oaths to support and defend various state constitutions and municipal or county charters during my thirty-four years of wearing the badge of a municipal, county, and federal law enforcement officer. Even before I took the first of those oaths, I had committed my life to an even higher authority. I surrendered my life to my Lord and Savior, Jesus Christ. In July of 1962, I became a Christian during a Christian Service Brigade youth organization summer campout at Lake Isabella in California. I had heard the message of salvation preached in a church environment for some months before this experience occurred, but I still needed to reach a point of conviction and brokenness in my life before I was willing to enlist in God's Army. It seems I have been some type of warrior my whole life ever since.

As I looked back on my life of service to my fellow man, there was one key difference I found between my three chosen professions. Before I was called "Marine," I decided to become one: I enlisted, I went through a very thorough recruit training, and then, and only then, did I earn the title "Marine." I went through a similar cycle of decision-making and training when I entered into the world of law enforcement. I would have to earn recognition by my performance here as well. The cycle changed, though, during the process of becoming a Christian. The same desire was there, but the motivation was different. The recognition and performance expectations came before the training. I had few role models and little support from my family and friends upon which to rely.

I have served my country and Corps in two theaters of operations: Southeast and Southwest Asia, between the years of 1963 and 1996. I have also patrolled the "mean streets" of seven different states. Because of my excellent training, I never felt like there was a situation I could not handle. However, I never expected to encounter the number of battles, or to deal with the frequency of conflict, or to enter into battle as quickly as I did as a Christian. I was totally unprepared, untrained, and attacked immediately. Throughout my careers, I have learned that no matter how long I was in the military service, law enforcement, or God's Army, my training in the arena of good and evil will never be complete.

Training is dynamic. As we learn more, we learn how much we really do not know. This alone should increase our appetite for additional training. If learning does not, then the realization that the spiritual warfare tactics we face are far beyond our own capabilities should convince even the most reluctant recruit to learn all he or she can. God provided both a basic and advanced training plan for each of us. They are found in an OPLAN (operations plan) called the Bible. Even though the plan is there for everyone to study and learn from, to try it on your own without any assistance would be as foolish as military trainees constituting the entire training staff during "boot camp" and in combat staging battalions. I needed and deserved the most experienced drill instructors to train me in the military and law enforcement academies I attended. Without those qualified instructors, I would more than likely have become a combat casualty. Training for spiritual combat without the guidance and direction of the Holy Spirit is just as dangerous, imprudent, and fruitless.

In no way, however, should this manuscript be viewed as anything but a chronicle of the experiences Christ has used to influence and mold my life. I have won and lost many battles during my Christian life, and I have marched through many valleys where the shadow of death lay in wait. Even though I do not claim to be a mighty combat leader in God's Task Force, I am willing to accept whatever leadership role the Holy Spirit places me in. My current mission orders appear to be to continue as Christ's servant and to undertake the development of this spiritual basic training manual. I can only think of one response to those orders: "Aye, Aye, Sir," a response I was taught in boot camp that means, "I understand, and I will obey!"

Mission

It is my sole intent that as you journey through the book of Ephesians in the following pages, you study it in light of my experiences and the understanding of spiritual combat with which My Lord and Savior has equipped me. Please rely on the Holy Spirit to enlighten you as you search for the truth through what he has taught me. I hope that by narrating your trip through this manuscript—as though you were sitting around between battles as Paul, Christ, and I discuss it—that this effort will help you to gain maturity and appreciation for your Christian walk and that you may more readily understand the concerns and advice Paul was inspired to write to the early Church at Ephesus. This wisdom is still applicable today. You will notice that I quite frequently use singular pronouns to personalize many portions of this manuscript. This is intentional. The Bible and its contents must be taken personally, a fact that seems to be overlooked all too frequently. May God bless this endeavor undertaken for His glory.

Now listen to the following SitRep (situation report), and let's get this party started!

SitRep (Situation Report) Ephesus

It was after the reign of Augustus that the buildings of Ephesus we admire today were constructed. According to some sources, the city was severely damaged in an earthquake in AD 17. After that, however, Ephesus was rebuilt into a very important center of trade and commerce. The historian Aristio describes Ephesus as the most important trading center in Asia during its heyday. It was also the leading political and intellectual center, hosting the second school of philosophy in the Aegean region. From the first century on, Ephesus was visited by Christian disciples who attempted to spread the Christian belief in a single God and were often forced to seek refuge from Roman persecution.

Besides enjoying a privileged position between East and West and an exceptionally fine climate, the city was important because it was the center for the cult of Artemis.

The goddess Artemis played a captivating role in Greek mythology and religion. She was known as the mistress of animals and the protectress of children, but she was also a huntress and a goddess who could bring death with her arrows. Artemis was an uncompromising and dominant goddess, a female who could punish injustices against the gods with ferocious and deadly accuracy. Artemis was the daughter of Leto and Zeus (the ruler of the Greek gods). With her twin brother, Apollo, she enjoyed the rank and privileges of an Olympian, which meant she was free to pursue her interests. She was often found frolicking in the forests accompanied by a band of nymphs and young human women sworn to virginity. Artemis is associated with the ancient Egyptian goddess Bast, as well as the Roman goddess Diana. Artemis is also often associated with the goddesses Luna, Hecate, and Selene.

For the Christians, the city—with its highly advanced way of life, its high standard of living, the variety of its demographic composition, and its firmly rooted polytheistic culture—must have presented itself as fertile ground for their missionary outreach.

From written sources, we learn that Paul remained in the city for three years, from AD 65 to 68, and that it was here that he preached his sermons, calling upon people to embrace the faith in one God. He taught that God had no need of a house made with human hands, and that He was present in all places at all times. This Gospel was greatly resented by many of the craftsmen who had amassed great wealth from their production of statues of Artemis in gold, silver, or other materials. When Paul's teaching began to affect their income, a silversmith named Demetrius stirred up the people and led a crowd of thousands of Ephesians to the theater where Paul was preaching. The crowd booed and tried to stone Paul and his two colleagues, chanting, "Great is Artemis of the Ephesians! Great is Artemis of the Ephesians!" So turbulent was the crowd that Paul and his companions escaped only with great difficulty.

From his epistles to the various churches, you could correctly deduce that Paul spent some time as a prisoner in Ephesus.

There is also a legend that John the Evangelist came to Ephesus with Mary, Jesus' mother, in his care. Some theologians feel that it was here that John wrote his Gospel and was finally buried.

In 269 Ephesus and the surrounding countryside were devastated by the Goths. At that time there was still a temple to Artemis. In 381, by order of the Emperor Theodosius, this temple was closed down, and in the following centuries it lay completely abandoned, serving merely as a quarry for building materials.

Now as you begin your investigation into a book of the Bible that is claimed by many Christians as their favorite, you will see that, though the book is merely six chapters, this journey will take quite some time.

But before your training begins in earnest, let's look closely at Paul's relationship with the Christian "Firebase Ephesus," and his message to its resident Christian soldiers.

His message, while useful for all Christians, was originally directed to the Church at Ephesus. If you wonder why, you may not be aware that Paul had a history with the city. Near the end of Paul's second missionary journey, he passed through Ephesus and, as he related in Acts 18:19–21, "entered the synagogue and reasoned with the Jews, and when they asked him to stay for a longer time, he did not consent, but taking leave of them and saying, 'I will return to you again if God wills,' he then sailed from Ephesus." Paul later found time to return to Ephesus. When he returned, "he entered the synagogue and continued speaking out boldly for three months, reasoning and persuading [them] about the kingdom of God. But when some were becoming hardened and disobedient, speaking evil of the Way before the multitude, he withdrew from them" (Acts 19:8–9).

Though he stayed longer this time, they didn't want to hear from him because he had upset their status quo. So choosing his battleground and abandoning the temple, Paul took these new Christians with him, rented a school, and continued to preach the Gospel in Ephesus for two years. Armies of people were saved, both Jews and Gentiles, and added to the Church. God was performing miracles of healing through Paul: demons were being cast out of people (Acts 19:12), and some magicians and witches were repenting, proclaiming their faith in Christ and burning their occult books (Acts 19:19). Such large numbers of people were turning from their wicked beliefs that the tradesmen and silversmiths who made their living making and selling idols of Artemis began to riot and denounce Paul and his teachings because they were losing money and being put out of business. The uproar created by his teaching, which forced Paul to leave Ephesus, is described in Acts 20:1. Paul's final departure from the Ephesians did not even occur in Ephesus. He had to sail to Miletus. From there he called for the leadership of the Ephesian Church to discuss the ramifications of his forced exodus. Upon their arrival he met with them and exhorted them diligently to guard the flock, to watch out for wolves (false teachers and prophets), to be consistently alert, and further admonishing them to teach the Word. After he prayed with them, he once again embarked on his ship and headed off.

When we get underway, remember what I said. All of Paul's teaching is as relevant to the present-day Church and to each of us personally as it was to the Ephesians when he wrote it.

All right troops fall in! You've got the picture; so let's get motivated. Show me some life out there. We have a long way to go and time is critical, so let's not waste any. As our training begins, the time is near AD 63, and Paul is writing from the same Roman prison where he previously dictated his dispatches to Philemon and the Colossians.

1

1:1 Paul's Credentials

> "Paul, an apostle of Jesus Christ by the will of God, to the saints,
> which are at Ephesus, and to the faithful in Christ Jesus." (Eph. 1:1)

When a Command Special Order is issued, it must contain information regarding who is issuing it, under whose authority it is being issued, and to whom it applies. Similarly, the first thing to be written in a letter during Paul's era was the sender's identity and a greeting. Therefore, it stands to reason that in this document, Paul should identify himself in the very beginning of Ephesians, where he also describes his commission as an apostle. He does not do this with any arrogance or pride. On the contrary, he points out that he only holds this position "by the will of God." In other words, Paul is saying he doesn't have a choice in the matter. God gave him his mission and his marching orders, and, like any good soldier, he was executing them. But for those who may be babes in Christ, before we go too far, we need to pause a moment to review Paul's conversion and salvation experience.

When the Lord first called Paul, he was known as Saul of Tarsus, a highly respected Pharisee. You see, Paul was one of approximately 6,000 existing Pharisees at the time, a very small number. He was well educated in Jewish law and an enthusiastic persecutor of Christians. He was struck down on the road to Damascus, where he was heading to take more Christians into custody, and blinded by a resurrected Jesus. God then told Ananias, a disciple at Damascus, to go to a certain house on Straight Street and pray for this blinded persecutor of the Church. Ananias understandably balked a bit, but God reassured him. In Acts 9:15–16, He said, "Go, for he is a chosen instrument of Mine, to bear My name before the Gentiles and kings and the sons of Israel; for I will show him how much he must suffer for My name's sake," Ananias

1

wisely complied. Paul's sight was subsequently restored, as was Paul himself. Paul continued to acknowledge throughout his ministry that his apostleship was God's will, not his own. You see this again when Paul tells the Corinthians in 1 Corinthians 9:16, "For if I preach the Gospel, I have nothing to boast of, for I am under compulsion; for woe is me if I do not preach the Gospel."

Paul Is an Apostle of Christ Jesus

Notice that Paul says he is an "apostle of Christ Jesus." Paul is carrying a message of truth, and Jesus, who is the truth, must be the focus of any message we proclaim. He Himself tells us He is The Way, The Truth, and The Life that we are to make known to the world. Paul said in 1 Corinthians 2:2, "For I determined to know nothing among you except Jesus Christ, and Him crucified." While today there are many witnesses and messengers proclaiming to be carrying all kinds of spiritual truths and revelations—including Jehovah's Witnesses going door-to-door proclaiming Jehovah—I, like Paul, am determined to count myself as one of Jesus' committed witnesses. Who are you witnessing for?

Who Are the Saints and the Faithful?

Since Paul seems to be writing "to the saints who are at Ephesus, and [who are] faithful in Christ Jesus," I might need to clarify just whom he is talking about when he uses the term "saints." There have been many debates throughout history regarding the implications of the term "saints." Biblically, saints are not extremely scrupulous people who have been set apart by theological authorities in some specific denominations of the Church as extra-special Christians. Acts 9:13, 32, and 41 all point out quite clearly that saints are truly born-again Christians. The term applies to everyone who has placed his or her faith in Jesus Christ. Paul told the Galatians in Galatians 3:26, "You are all sons of God through faith in Christ Jesus." So if today you can confess Jesus as your Lord and Savior, and you truly believe in your heart that God raised Him from the dead, then you too are a saint, a holy and set-apart child of God. By virtue of that relationship, you are also an enlistee in the Army of Christ.

It is also important that, while still in the early stages of your mission, you realize that Paul's writings are as applicable to the Church today as they were to the Ephesian Church at the time he penned them. The Holy Spirit, you must remember, inspired Paul's words and writings. These are, beyond any shadow of a doubt, the words of God himself.

1:2 Grace and Peace: A "Call-Sign" of Paul?

"Grace [be] to you, and peace, from God our Father, and [from] the Lord Jesus Christ." (Eph. 1:2)

All of Paul's epistles contain the greeting, "Grace to you and peace." Some Christians have, for that reason, discounted this as simply Paul's way of conveying his hellos to the Greeks and the Hebrews. But since it is such an integral part of Paul's correspondence—almost like a radio call sign is fundamental to all military and law enforcement radio transmitted message traffic, I trust its designed purpose is to call to your attention to so much more. For it is by the grace of Jesus Christ that we are saved, as we are told in Acts 15:11. The Bible also records in Romans 5:1, "Therefore having been justified by faith; we have peace with God through our Lord Jesus Christ." Ephesians 2:8 says, "Grace comes to us through faith in Him." So when Paul writes, "Grace to you and peace," he is reminding you that because you believe in Jesus Christ, you have received an absolutely unearned gift: everlasting life. You are a friend of God! The separation and antagonism separating you and God are gone. You have become the recipient of peace with God and peace in yourselves, a peace that passes all understanding and is the direct result of unjustifiable grace.

1:3 Our Spiritual Blessing

"Blessed [be] the God and Father of our Lord Jesus Christ, who hath blessed us with all spiritual blessings in heavenly [places] in Christ." (Eph. 1:3)

Verse 3 actually begins a Greek sentence that does not end until verse 14. Some people might say that Paul was the master of notation without vacillation! (that means the run-on sentence.) Some of you reading this book may soon feel I am a worthy competitor of Paul. It would not surprise me if he seldom took a breath when he began speaking about the blessings of God! But let us go back and look at verse three alone for right now.

Paul says in Ephesians 1:3 that God has "blessed us with every spiritual blessing in the heavenly [places] in Christ." I want you to notice the use of the past tense. God has already blessed you! He's already awarded you citizenship in Heaven, as is evidenced in Philippians 3:20, and He's causing all things to work together for good here on earth. You might want to also take a look at Romans 8:28.

Blessed Be

It is a fact, whether or not you concede to it, that God has already blessed us with more than we generally acknowledge, and here Paul reminds us that we are negligent when we fail to exalt Him for doing this. Our challenge every morning is to consider whether others will view our daily actions as blessing God. Do you appear thankful? Do you exhibit a proper and worshipful attitude? Do you acknowledge that, as it says in James 1:17, "Every good thing bestowed and every perfect gift is from above, coming down from the Father"? I pray that you will always bless God for blessing you.

Selah (Take your gear off for ten and pause and reflect.)

Up to now we have discussed some of the history Paul had with the Ephesians and some of the conditions that existed during the time he wrote this letter to them. We have only covered three verses, yet we have had an opportunity to deal with several major topics, including the source of his apostolic commission, which you learned was a direct commission by the will of God, not one of his own initiative. He did not choose the path he was on but God chose it for him. In fact, the Lord affirmed in Acts 9:15, "He is a chosen instrument of Mine." Remember, Paul did not personally seek his apostleship; he even indicated at other times that he was under compulsion (1 Cor. 9:16).

Coming up, we'll look at the radical and controversial topic of God's right to choose, not only Paul, but also each and every one of us. Does that sound a bit like the draft? Well saddle up and lets get started, we're burning daylight.

1:4–12 The Battle of Predestination

"According as he hath chosen us in him before the foundation of the world, that we should be holy and without blame before him in love: Having predestinated us unto the adoption of children by Jesus Christ to himself, according to the good pleasure of his will, To the praise of the glory of his grace, wherein he hath made us accepted in the beloved. In whom we have redemption through his blood, the forgiveness of sins, according to the riches of his grace; Wherein he hath abounded toward us in all wisdom and prudence; Having made known unto us the mystery of his will, according to his good pleasure which he hath purposed in himself: That in the dispensation of the fullness of times he might gather together in one all things in Christ, both which are in heaven, and which are on earth; [even] in him: In whom also we have obtained an inheritance, being predestinated according to the purpose of him who worketh all things after the counsel of his own will: That we should be to the praise of his glory, who first trusted in Christ." (Eph. 1:4–12)

I was not saved until my middle teens. Consequently, I was not raised in church and had little spiritual training, though I had been exposed to the Gospel in many different settings. Thus I did have somewhat of a multidenominational veneer when I finally came to understand my relationship with Christ. When I read what the Bible had to say about predestination, I had formed no precise opinion of its validity or of the controversy surrounding it. I had no definite point of view as to whether this doctrine should be questioned, embraced, or denied. Now that I have been a Christian for almost forty-one years, I have found that predestination is a topic that can make even the most docile Christian or Non-Christian folks somewhat hot under the collar. It seems as though some Christians can never accept the fact that both man's free will and God's sovereignty can co-exist within a single philosophy. Heaven help those folks when they start to study the complexities of the Holy Trinity.

I could spend weeks going over detailed arguments for both sides of this issue, and the destructive results of siding with either of these extreme positions. Instead, I want to simply point out four things that you should be able to glean from this section of Scripture: (1) the fact that God does predestine; (2) His motive for doing it; (3) who is predestined; and (4) the effect it has on you.

(1) He Chose Us in Him

If you read these verses without allowing yourself to be swayed by someone's denominational dogma, you can plainly see what the Scripture says:

"...He chose us in Him before the foundation of the world." (Eph. 1:4)

"He predestined us to adoption as sons." (Eph. 1:5)

"His will...which He purposed." (Eph. 1:9)

"Having been predestined according to His purpose who works all things after the counsel of His will." (Eph. 1:11)

This looks like a clear declaration that God predestined your salvation long before you were born. He chose you to be His child before the world was made. No matter how you slice it or dice or analyze it, it is as uncomplicated as Jesus said in John 15:16, "You did not choose Me, but I chose you, and appointed you." Throughout the Scriptures, we can see that God has often done this. He chose the people of Israel corporately. He chose Abraham (Neh. 9:7), David (Ps. 78:70), and Solomon (1 Chr. 28:5) individually. Psalm 47:4 says, "He chooses our inheritance for us." Paul told the Thessalonians in 2 Thessalonians 2:13, "God has chosen you from the beginning for salvation through sanctification by the Spirit and faith in the truth."

It is clear God picked you, chose you, and predestined you to be saved. Most folks might still be in agreement at this point, but wait until we reach checkpoint three.

Bear with me, and let's check out God's motivation for doing this.

(2) In His Love

God's motives for predestination are pretty obvious throughout these passages:

"In love He predestined us." (Eph. 1:4–5)

"According to the kind intention of His will." (Eph. 1:5)

"His grace, which He freely bestowed on us." (Eph. 1:6)

"According to the riches of His grace, which He lavished upon us." (Eph. 1:7–8)

"According to His kind intention." (Eph. 1:9)

There is never a reason for any of us to be upset with the Lord, especially over the question of predestination. Predestination is simply more evidence that He really loves us completely, He wants to bless us abundantly, and He is graceful and good consistently. It is my well-thought-out opinion that God has predestined you for salvation because He loves you. Consider that for a moment, will you? What does it mean for you? What is the result? Is everyone still aboard? Good, but standby for our next exercise.

(3) Who Does This Predestination Apply to?

I am about to give you a clue, but I want you to "hang-fire" for a minute and we'll see if you pick up on it. O.K., I say it applies to all mankind, as we are told straightforwardly in John 3:16, "For God so loved the world that He gave His only begotten son, that whosoever should believe on him should not perish, but have everlasting life," and in John 3:17, "For God sent not His Son into the world to condemn the world, but that the world through Him might be saved." Let that sink in for a minute while you look at the last point.

(4) We Are Holy and Blameless before Him

And these are the outcomes of our being predestined:

"We should be holy and blameless before Him." (Eph. 1:4)
"Adoption as sons through Jesus Christ to Himself." (Eph. 1:5)
"We have redemption through His blood, the forgiveness of our trespasses." (Eph. 1:7)
"We have obtained an inheritance." (Eph. 1:11)

When you accept the salvation for which you have been predestined, you become a child of God. He makes you holy and blameless. He ransoms your life and forgives your sins. He promises you a heavenly inheritance. It is so overwhelming to think that God, knowing how rotten a person would behave, how sinful they would be, and how rebelliously they would act, chose them for eternal life anyway. That's how much He loves me, and that's how much He loves you.

The Battle of Predestination "Hot Wash" (Critique)

Well, now you know the benefits belonging to the predestined. But I know some of you are sitting here reading this and complaining, "Oh, so since I'm not a Christian, I guess that proves God hasn't predestined me; God doesn't love me; God doesn't care about me." What have you been doing? You have not been listening, I guess. The answers to those three questions are, no, no, and no! That is the great—though sometimes controversial—thing about this.

God has made His predestination obtainable by anyone that desires to trigger it. Remember, the Bible guarantees that in John 3:16. Read it again, slower if necessary, or as we say in boot camp, "By the numbers." "God so loved the world, that He gave His only begotten Son, that *whosoever* [clue: that means anyone] believes in Him should not perish, but have eternal life" (italics added for emphasis). Jesus also pointed out in John 6:37, "The one who comes to Me I will certainly not cast out." If you want to receive the forgiveness offered to all the predestined (and you now know that the offer is made to everyone), then all you need to do is do this. Be aware that you are a sinner, and your sin has separated you from God, and that His only Son Jesus died on the Cross to pay the price of your sin because He loves you so much. By His resurrection, He conquered death and won the war, guaranteeing Christians salvation and everlasting life with Him in His kingdom. You only need to ask God to forgive your sins, and you will discover that you too have been predestined, because God knew what choice you'd make long before you made it. After all, the predestined are merely those who have been "chosen according to the foreknowledge of God" (1 Pet. 1:1–2). "For whom He foreknew, He also predestined" (Rom. 8:29). Do you want eternal life? "Let the one who is thirsty come; let the one who wishes take the water of life without cost" (Rev. 22:17).

It is true God recognized before time began those who would choose to be adopted as sons and daughters into his family, but He does not relieve any man of his responsibility to believe the Gospel and make an individual choice in order to access or fulfill God's predestination. It is my firm belief and understanding that God does not intend for any person to be denied salvation and eternal life in Heaven. Therefore He would not, while knowing us before we were in the womb, prepare a plan for our lives that did not provide an opportunity for our acceptance of Christ as our personal Savior. Thus we are all predestined to reach a point in our lives where we have the responsibility to act on our own and accept or reject His precious opportunity. For those of you who accept it, your fate and mission are clear. You must carry the Gospel message in your lives as you live it for Your Father Who Art in Heaven.

A study of Ephesians can never take place without encountering many major biblical topics. We have just scratched the surface of this study, and we have already addressed the topic of predestination. Next we will probe the workings of the Holy Spirit.

So let's dive back in, since we're still burning daylight.

1:13–14 The Message of Truth

"In whom ye also [trusted], after that ye heard the word of truth, the Gospel of your salvation: in whom also after that ye believed, ye were sealed with that Holy Spirit of promise, Which is the earnest of our inheritance until the redemption of the purchased possession, unto the praise of his glory". (Eph. 1:13–14)

Before we go much further, we need to review your understanding of the word "Gospel." I have been taught many meanings for the word "Gospel." It has been defined as the truth, as, "God Offering Sinful People Eternal Life," and as the "Good News." A lot of people think it only refers to a kind of music, while others think that it is only a term for a specific book of the Bible written by Matthew, Mark, Luke, or John. I feel these are all apt definitions that may have application in their own circumstances. The basis for this good news is always the salvation and redemption offered by God through the death and resurrection of His only Son, Jesus Christ, something we will look more closely at as we progress on our journey. So let's tarry a moment longer and take a more in-depth look at the word "Gospel." and its entomology. In reality, the Greek word is pronounced *"yoo-ang-ghel-is-TACE"*, and it simply means good news. Similarly, the one who brings the Good News is called a *"yoo-ang-ghel-ID-zo"*, or, as we say in English, an evangelist. An evangelist is a messenger who brings the Good News, the Gospel.

I believe Greek and not Aramaic is the predominant language of the New Testament, though Aramaic idioms do seem to appear in some of the books. I believe this was caused, at least in part, by the regional use of dialects, accents, and local expressions that worked their way into the writings of God's chosen scribes.

Let's examine closer a question so many people ask: "What is the Gospel"? After all, even the Bible says that there are different Gospels. In Galatians 1:6, however, Paul warned that anyone who preached one of these different Gospels was accursed, and in Galatians 1:8–9, he said that his Gospel was tested by and consisted of each of the below:

Will one day judge men's secrets (Rom. 2:16)
-Jesus Christ (2 Tim. 2:8)

-The descendant of David (2 Tim. 2:8)

-Rose from the dead (2 Tim. 2:8)

-He was buried (1 Cor. 5:4)

-Who died for our sins (1 Cor. 15:3)

-On the third day (1 Cor. 15:4)

-He appeared publicly to many after His resurrection (1 Cor. 15:5–8)

You need to appreciate the fact that the Gospel is not merely information. While it truly is something to hear and then read, you must also, as it says in Acts 15:7, "Hear the word of the Gospel and believe." Only when you believe it are you saved. Romans 1:16 tells us, "The Gospel...is the power of God for salvation to everyone who believes." If you don't believe it, I'm sorry folks God says I can't mince words here, the Bible says you will die in your sin. 2 Corinthians 4:3 says, "If our Gospel is veiled, it is veiled to those who are perishing." It is primarily because of that veil that the work of evangelism was made a part of the calling of all Christians, and why it is so vitally important. This is, in a small way, like my Marine Corps saying, "No matter what your MOS, every Marine is basically a rifleman." Still, many Christians don't feel qualified to evangelize because they feel like they don't have a convincing personality. Many feel they don't have the necessary sales ability. This is why it is so imperative that you realize the Gospel isn't a convincing sales pitch. There is supernatural power behind it, a power drawing people to God and away from their sin. 1 Thessalonians 1:5 tells you, "For our Gospel did not come to you in word only, but also in power and in the Holy Spirit and with full conviction." The Word of the Gospel is powerful, and the Holy Spirit is dealing internally with the listener as you or I talk externally. Leave the hard work to God; your part is to be a FAT person. For God loves Faithful, Available, and Teachable people and accomplishes much through them.

The Holy Spirit

A lot of people seem to be confused about who or what the Holy Spirit is. Some folks think the Holy Spirit is only a force or a power. Some think the Holy Spirit is a ghost. But there is one vital and very simple fact that you need to remember: the Holy Spirit is God Himself. I hope you accept as true the principle that God has a threefold nature: Father, Son, and Holy Spirit. He is one God, yet He exists simultaneously as three distinct Persons. The Holy

Spirit is always mentioned by the pronoun "He." The Holy Spirit has three distinct relationships with people. First, He is to be next to them, drawing them into a relationship with Jesus Christ, convicting them of their sin, and bearing witness of Jesus Christ. Second, He lives in people when they accept Jesus as their personal Savior. This is why He is called "the Holy Spirit of promise," because Jesus promised Him to the disciples before they received Him. John 14:17 says, "He abides with you, and will be in you." He was next to them in John chapter 14, and would be in them in John chapter 20. And so Galatians 3:14 says that we "receive the promise of the Spirit through faith."

Third, He comes upon believers to empower them. This is a strange concept to many people, possibly even to you. This is probably because of the image created by current Charismatic and Pentecostal implications. I am not going to dwell on that issue here; we will have plenty of opportunities to study this in the upcoming chapters of Ephesians.

Receiving the Seal from the Holy Spirit

Right now, let's concentrate on that second work, the Holy Spirit being in people who believe. One of the most important reasons why He dwells inside of us is to seal us. What does a seal signify? To a Marine, it is the experience we go through the day the title of Marine is bestowed on us, at the end of recruit training and we are told we have earned the right to wear the Eagle, Globe, and Anchor, the mark of a U.S. Marine. Members of other armed forces also have a day when they are marked with a symbol of recognition that sets them apart from the crowd. It may be wings, a beret, a specific unit patch, crest, or some other award. Both a great deal of pride and responsibility are also inherited on this designation day. There is little difference for a Christian on the day they are born again in the faith. Biblically speaking. A seal is an impression put in clay (Job 38:14) signifying a royal decree, a mark of ownership, belonging, or of security. This was often applied to letters (as in 1 Kgs. 21:8; Est. 3:12, 8:8–10, documents in Neh. 9:38, books in Isa. 29:11; Rev. 5:1–9, deeds of purchase in Jer. 32:10–11, and even stone openings in Dan. 6:17; Matt. 27:66). But in addition to paper and stone, people can also be sealed, as we are told in Revelation 7:3–4. This sealing signifies God's royal decree that we are His. As Timothy states in 2 Timothy 2:19, "Having this seal, 'The Lord knows those who are His.'" In Ephesians 4:30, Paul writes, "The Holy Spirit of God, by whom you were sealed for the day of redemption." You have been set apart from the crowd, not that you should be filled with pride and boast, but that you should now train for and then act to fulfill the duties of your new profession as a soldier and messenger or ambassador of Christ. Just how well you perform these duties will determine whether others view your actions as reasons to become Christians or excuses not to become Christians. Remember, you are never operationally alone in this endeavor; the Holy Spirit is with you every step of the way.

Word of Honor of Our Inheritance

This seal of ownership is a pledge of our inheritance. Different translations of the Bible may refer to the Holy Spirit as a guarantee or a deposit. "The Holy Spirit is a deposit or first installment from God on our purchase; He might be likened to earnest money. Earnest money is a token payment assuring the recipient that the full amount will eventually follow from the purchaser. It can also be likened to giving one's intended an engagement ring" (*Expositor's Bible Commentary*). In the same way, a man gives his fiancée an engagement ring or a buyer puts earnest money down on a house, God has presented us His Holy Spirit as our constant companion and Comforter as a guarantee of our redemption. Romans 8:16 states, "The Spirit Himself bears witness with our spirit that we are children of God." If you check, you'll find Paul wrote the Corinthians, saying in 2 Corinthians 1:21–22, "Now He who establishes us with you in Christ and anointed us is God, who also sealed us and gave [us] the Spirit in our hearts as a pledge." God has promised us that we are His children.

Listening to (Not Just Hearing) the Message

A great many of you have heard the Gospel at some time in your life. Let me assure you it is a message of complete truth, and those of you who have responded to it and believed it have been sealed with the Holy Spirit. God's pledge to you is that you are His child and that you have an inheritance waiting for you in Heaven. But some of you may have never clearly understood that message of total truth. Well, for those of you who find yourselves claiming that category, here it is one more time as clearly as I can state it:

Jesus Christ is the Son of God and one part of the Trinity of God. He came to earth as a human being and was born to a virgin named Mary, who was a descendant of Israel's King David. His earthly birthright is to be the King of Israel. His divine birthright is to be the King of the entire universe. Although He never did a single thing wrong, He was tortured, was nailed to a cross, and was crucified. He died and was buried. He allowed this to happen so that through His death He could pay the penalty that your sins deserve. (The wages of sin, which is death Rom. 6:23). Three days later, He rose from the dead and appeared to more than 500 people over the course of forty days to confirm his resurrection with eyewitnesses. He then ascended up to Heaven, where He currently sits at the right hand of God the Father, a position from which He will one day judge people for their sins. But if you truly believe in Him, the Holy Spirit has sealed you and you will not be judged; you will be welcomed into Heaven. That, my friend, is the message of truth known as the Gospel. You've read it, now it's time to act on it, believe it, and be redeemed.

The concept of redemption can be described in three ideas:

1.   The blood of Christ paid the ransom for our eternal lives (1 Cor. 6:20 and Rev. 5:9).

2.   We were removed from the curse of the law (Gal. 3:13; 4:5).

3.   By grace we were released from the bondage of sin (Eph. 1:7; 1 Pet. 1:18).

Selah (Take your gear off for ten and pause and reflect.)

As we continue your verse-by-verse training in Ephesians, I promise you that we will encounter many more major Bible topics. Some will be controversial, and others will merely be difficult to understand, but we will persevere like the good soldiers we are becoming. The next subject can, I think, be accurately described with three adjectives: major, controversial, and difficult. So let's saddle up, move out, and get crackin'.

1:15–17 Motivation for Communication

"...wherefore I also, after I heard of your faith in the Lord Jesus, and love unto all the saints, Cease not to give thanks for you, making mention of you in my prayers; That the God of our Lord Jesus Christ, the Father of glory, may give unto you the spirit of wisdom and revelation in the knowledge of him". (Eph. 1: 15–17)

Paul has just finished telling you the Holy Spirit sealed the Ephesians when they heard and believed the Gospel. And he has told them, "For this reason, I thank God for you and pray for you all the time." After a little consideration, it is understandable why Paul tells them that he is praying they receive a spirit of wisdom and revelation.

However, it is the description of who Paul is asking that remains an obscurity to many. He is praying to "the God of our Lord Jesus Christ, the Father of Glory" (Eph. 1:17). This seems to confuse some people. After all, if Jesus is God, how can He have a God? And if He has a God, then He Himself can't be God, can He? But, if He's not God, then how can He be our God and Savior? It is certainly understandable, when you stop and reflect for a moment, how some people can misinterpret that Scripture, because the Holy Trinity of God is beyond many people's limited understanding.

I'm going to target in on those three questions I've just mentioned and show how:

1. Jesus is God

2. Jesus has a God

3. How these two facts mesh, and what it means to you.

Our Lord Jesus Christ.

Jesus is called, "Our Lord Jesus Christ." In fact, many people only want to interpret the word "Lord" to mean "God," when in fact the word is actually a respectful title meaning, master, possessor, and owner. It comes from a root word meaning "supremacy." Even though it is routinely applied to God and 99 percent of the time appropriately so, it is also a title that people used to refer to those to whom they were in submission. Read Colossians 4:1 and 1 Peter 3:6. So that He is called Lord is not bearing witness solely to His deity, but also to His supremacy, mastery, and ownership of mankind.

However, Jesus is not just Lord, He is also God. Thomas, when seeing and touching Jesus after His resurrection, proclaimed in John 20:28, "My Lord and my God!" Jesus in response, neither rebuked nor corrected him. Because Jesus was always known to tell the truth, if He were not both Lord and God, he would have had to say, "Lord, yes, But God? No!" Instead, He said those who didn't have the privilege of seeing but still believed were blessed. Thomas was not the only one to proclaim that Jesus is God. The Apostle John also did, when he wrote in John 1:1, "In the beginning was the Word, and the Word was with God, and the Word was God." Paul also testified to Jesus' deity when he said that you are "looking for the blessed hope and the appearing of the glory of our great God and Savior, Christ Jesus" (Titus 2:13). Simon Peter also called Him in 2 Peter 1:1, "Our God and Savior, Jesus Christ." Jesus' enemies pointed out that He Himself claimed to be God in John 10:33, "You, being a man, make yourself out to be God." Nor was it just the claims of Thomas, John, Paul, Peter, and Jesus. God Himself said that Jesus is God. Hebrews 1:8, 10 quotes God as saying this, "But of the Son He says, THY THRONE, O GOD, IS FOREVER AND EVER...And, THOU, LORD, IN THE BEGINNING DIDST LAY THE FOUNDATION OF THE EARTH, AND THE HEAVENS ARE THE WORKS OF THY HANDS."

So, as we can see, God (the Father) also called Jesus, "God" and "Lord." You can also see the demonstration of Jesus as God in His actions. As you've just read, He created everything (John 1:3; Col. 1:16). And the Bible clearly says in Genesis 1:1, "In the beginning God created the heavens and the earth." Jesus created everything; God created everything. He also forgave sins. Mark 2:7 states, "Who can forgive sins but God alone?" Additionally, we can see His divinity in His titles. For example, God said in Isaiah 44:6, "I am the first and I am the last, and there is no God besides Me." While Jesus says in Revelation 22:13, "I am the Alpha and the Omega, the first and the last, the beginning and the end."

Yes, my friend, the Scriptures are quite clear: Jesus Christ is God.

Who Then Is the God of Jesus?

Now let me completely confuse you. Jesus Christ has a God. All through Jesus' earthly ministry, He said He was here to submit to God, to do God's will, and to obey God. He called God His "Father," and always pointed out that He was not the Father but the Son. Listen to these things that Jesus said:

"All that the Father gives Me shall come to Me, and the one who comes to Me I will certainly not cast out. For I have come down from heaven, not to do My own will, but the will of Him who sent Me. And this is the will of Him who sent Me" (John 6:37–38).

"He who sent Me is true; and the things which I heard from Him, these I speak to the world...and I do nothing on My own initiative, but I speak these things as the Father taught Me. And He who sent Me is with Me; He has not left Me alone, for I always do the things that are pleasing to Him" (John 8:26, 28–29).

"If anyone loves Me, he will keep My word; and My Father will love him, and We will come to him, and make Our abode with him" (John 14:23).

"Just as the Father has loved Me, I have also loved you; abide in My love. If you keep My commandments, you will abide in My love; just as I have kept My Father's commandments, and abide in His love" (John 15:9–10).

After Jesus rose from the dead, Mary was holding onto Him. In John 20:17, Jesus said to her, "Stop clinging to Me, for I have not yet ascended to the Father; but go to My brethren, and say to them, 'I ascend to My Father and your Father, and My God and your God.'"

All of these references clearly portray Jesus as not being the same person as the Father:

- The Father gave to the Son.

- The Son submitted to and obeyed the Father.

- The Son came to do the Father's will.

- The Father sent the Son.

- The Son heard from the Father.

- The Son talked to us about the Father.

- The Father taught the Son.

- The Father did not leave the Son alone.

- The Son did what was pleasing to the Father

After reading these things, there can be no argument that Jesus and the Father were the same Person; these are clearly two separate Persons. Yet they are definitely one as well.

Why Both Truths?

I have shown you beyond a shadow of a doubt that Jesus has a God: the Father. And yet just a moment ago, we conclusively proved that Jesus is God. Since they are both clear truths in the Word of God, they both must be true, and yet how can we accept both of those things as being true when they seem so incompatible?

I have heard a great many attempts to illustrate the Trinity. "God is like an egg—one egg, three parts: shell, white, and yolk." "God is like water—one thing in three forms: ice, water, and steam." "God made us in His image, and we are body, soul, and spirit."

Candidly, these are all grievously flawed illustrations. And yet, as an instructor, I feel obligated to try and take complicated ideas and make them simple enough for anyone to understand. I once heard a young girl give a very simple explanation of this truth, as she understood it. Her response was, "It's not simple, and it can't be. If God were that easy for man to understand, then He wouldn't be God." The truth is, you can never truly understand the concept of God's three-in-one nature as Father, Son, and Holy Spirit, any more than we can comprehend God's righteousness, His glory, His power, His perfection, or His love. The simple fact is that you and I are too simple to understand God completely.

The Bible says that one day you will get it. 1 John 3:2 says, "We know that, when He appears, we shall be like Him, because we shall see Him just as He is." But until that day when you see Him face to face, you must simply accept some truths, even though you cannot comprehend them.

I do want to point out, however, something the Bible does make absolutely clear, something that you can understand and must apply. Philippians 2:5–11 says:

> Have this attitude in yourselves which was also in Christ Jesus, who, although He existed in the form of God, did not regard equality with God a thing to be grasped, but emptied Himself, taking the form of a bond-servant, [and] being made in the likeness of men. And being found in appearance as a man, He humbled Himself by becoming obedient to the point of death, even death on a cross. Therefore also God highly exalted Him, and bestowed on Him the name that is above every name, that at the name of Jesus *every knee should bow*, of those who are in heaven, and on earth, and under the earth, and that every tongue should confess that Jesus Christ is Lord, to the glory of God the Father. (Italics added for emphasis)

As an American and a human being, you are more than likely very concerned with your rights, getting what you deserve, and not letting anyone walk all over you. It often seems like nobody has ever heard of another word that starts with the letter "R". I'm talking about responsibility! But Jesus is your example. Although He was in total power, deserved all rights and privileges, and was in the primary position of authority, He did not hold onto that. Instead, He made Himself low. He emptied Himself of His rights. He was obedient to the Father. He became a servant of man. He even let Himself be nailed to the Cross and killed. He was motivated to do this by His love for each of us. "For God so loved the world, that He gave His only begotten Son, that whoever believes in Him should not perish, but have eternal life" (John 3:16). There is a military saying about this; in fact there are several that seem to apply here. I have heard my peers and even superiors parroting these phrases they have heard throughout their careers, but I often wondered if they really understood them. Things like, "Rank has its privileges," or "First in garrison, but last in the field." I have even experienced the impact of those who didn't realize that "rank also has its *responsibilities*," and when a man puts himself above others, his position is much more precarious than that of a man who is lifted to new heights on the shoulders of admiring subordinates. These self-centered people also seem to have missed Christ's message that teaches He who would be first must be last, and the humble will be exalted. In all my years of service, seldom if ever did I see a commander carried aloft and respected by subordinates whom he walked all over to gain his success. I have seen, on the other hand, troops who would charge the gates of hell for a strong and benevolent commander who treated his troops with respect, caring for their needs above his own. Respect, like God's gifts, cannot be earned; it must be freely given. We are all sinners, but God loves us and paid the price of our sin. Jesus Christ, God the Son and the Son of God, died on Mount Calvary in our place, and if we believe in Him, we will have eternal life. Jesus showed us the true meaning of responsibility when He said, "Not My will, but Thy will be done."

Selah (Take your gear off for ten and pause and reflect.)

Paul has been uplifting the Ephesians by telling them that he has been praying for them. Specifically, he has been praying that they will be given "a spirit of wisdom and of revelation in the knowledge of God (the Father)" (Eph. 1:17). Paul wanted them to increase their knowledge of God and to advance their understanding of God and of all of the blessings He has made available to anyone who commits their life to Christ. It was Paul's fervent desire that every Christian—including those who find themselves reading or studying this text today—acquire this higher level of perception.

OK, troops, it's time to mount up and move out. We need to look at three more things we should understand in greater depth as we continue to cultivate our knowledge of God.

1:18–19a An Enlightened Heart

"The eyes of your understanding being enlightened; that ye may know what is the hope of his calling, and what the riches of the glory of his inheritance in the saints, And what [is] the exceeding greatness of his power to us-ward who believe". (Eph. 1:18–19a)

Paul prayed that the Ephesians would grow to know God in a more personal way, that the eyes of their hearts would be opened. Some of you may be familiar with the praise chorus "Open the Eyes of My Heart." Only when our heart's eyes are truly opened can we really begin to see the things that are revealed to us. I have heard it said before that there are many pseudo-Christians who will miss Heaven by about eighteen inches, because that is the distance between their heads and their hearts. You can possess all the head knowledge of the Bible that man can acquire, but if that knowledge of the following ideas are not working within your heart, you have not understood anything you learned:

1.   The hope of His calling

2.   The riches of the glory of His inheritance in the saints

3.   The surpassing greatness of His power

What do you say we look at these three in a little more detail.

How Do You Recognize the Hope of His Calling?

As the eyes of your heart are opened, you will begin to detect what the hope of His calling really means. The calling Paul is speaking of is a holy and a heavenly calling. The Bible says in 2 Timothy 1:9 that God "has saved us, and called us with a holy calling, not according to our works, but according to His own purpose and grace."

God called you to be His child. He chose you, not because you were holy or had a fantastic C.V. of good works, or even because you displayed enormous potential. The fact of the matter is, the Father called you in order that He might demonstrate His grace, his undeserved favor. In other words, God didn't call you to be Christians because you were so good; quite the contrary, He chose you because you were so bad! He did this so that anyone who notices the radical transformation in your life (a shifting from unholy activities to holy activities) has to acknowledge, "Only God could do that!"

Your calling is not only holy, but also heavenly. In Hebrews 3:1, you learn that you are "partakers of a heavenly calling." When you begin to consider the heavenly part of your calling, you start to realize just how wonderful the hope of His calling is. 1 Corinthians 2:9 says, "Eye has not seen and ear has not heard, and have not entered the heart of man, all that God has prepared for those who love him." Every time I read that verse, I just want to bust out in that old chorus, "Eyes have seen, ears have heard, it's recorded in God's Word, isn't Jesus my Lord wonderful." Sorry 'about that. On second thought, no I'm not;, I am a happy Christian wandering through a foreign land, and I take pleasure from spreading joy whenever I can. The fact that you didn't have to hear me really sing that chorus should really fill you with joy.

Nobody can even imagine how great Heaven will be! No matter how close to Paradise you may think you have come in this corrupt world, that experience will pale in comparison to the hope of our heavenly calling. Reflect for a few moments on what God's Word tells us about Heaven:

> "In Thy presence is fullness of joy; In Thy right hand there are pleasures forever." (Ps. 16:11)
>
> "Neither can they die anymore, for they are like angels, and are sons of God." (Luke 20:36)
>
> "They shall hunger no more, neither thirst anymore; neither shall the sun beat down on them, nor any heat; for the Lamb in the center of the throne shall be their shepherd, and shall guide them to springs of the water of life; and God shall wipe every tear from their eyes." (Rev. 7:16–17)
>
> "And there shall no longer be [any] night; and they shall not have need of the light of a lamp nor the light of the sun, because the Lord God shall illumine them; and they shall reign forever and ever." (Rev. 22:5)

We will experience anything even remotely like this on earth. Such is the hope of your heavenly calling.

What Are the Riches of His Inheritance?

When your heart's eyes begin to open, you learn about the riches of the glory of God's inheritance in the saints. But what does that mean? First of all, there are two ways to read this in the Greek language. It can be understood to say that you are God's inheritance, meaning you belong to Him, or it can be understood to say that God gave you an inheritance. Either translation would be valid, but in the context of these verses, along with the way that Paul speaks about inheritance in the rest of Ephesians, I believe it becomes clear that this is speaking of your inheritance.

> "In Him also we have obtained an inheritance." (Eph. 1:10–11)
> "The Holy Spirit of promise, who is given as a pledge of our inheritance." (Eph. 1:13–14)
> "No immoral or impure person or covetous man, who is an idolater, has an inheritance in the kingdom." (Eph. 5:5)

At the end of a soldier's career, he is rewarded for meritorious service with a retirement package. You, as a Christian Soldier, also have a retirement package awaiting you at the end of your earthly battles; it is an inheritance in the Kingdom of God. As the eyes of your heart are opened, you will begin to recognize that while most people in this world are futilely striving for its fleeting and temporal riches and glory, the glory and the riches you will receive in Heaven are eternal. Peter said that you will "obtain an inheritance, which is imperishable and undefiled and will not fade away, reserved in heaven for you" (1 Pet. 1:4). Jesus called these riches in Luke 12:33, "Purses which do not wear out, an unfailing treasure in heaven, where no thief comes near, nor moth destroys."

It's comforting to know that although the stock market can crash, the economy can take a nosedive, or your home or bank can be robbed, the glorious inheritance you have waiting for you in Heaven is forever secure.

Discerning the Surpassing Greatness of God's Power

When you receive this enlightening information, you will begin to realize God's power can only be accurately described as "surpassing greatness." The amazing thing is not just that God is powerful, but that He directs His power toward you. You may recall having been told in Ephesians 3:20, "He is able to do exceeding abundantly beyond all that we ask or think, according to the power that works within us." Those of you who have placed your faith in Christ have all the power of God available to you! This is why you are told in Romans 8:28, "We know that God causes all things to work together for good to those who love God, to those who are called according to [His] purpose." And it is also why Isaiah 54:17 says, "No weapon that is formed against you shall prosper." This power will bring about your resurrection to eternal life, for the Bible says in 1 Corinthians 6:14, "Now God has not only raised the Lord, but will also raise us up through His power."

1:19b–20 Strength in Christ

"According to the working of his mighty power, Which he wrought in Christ, when he raised him from the dead, and set [him] at his own right hand in the heavenly [places]". (Eph. 1:19b–20)

All three of these things we have just covered: the heavenly calling, the riches of your inheritance, and the power given you, were brought about when Christ rose from the dead and you became believers in His resurrection.

I don't want to seem like an elitist, but if you aren't a Marine, you aren't a Marine. Likewise, if you haven't yet put your trust in Jesus Christ, you aren't a Christian. Therefore the opposite is true. You do not have the hope of Heaven, a rich inheritance, or God's power working in your life. But it doesn't have to remain that way. All you need to do to receive these things is to recognize that your sin has separated you from God, and believe that Jesus Christ, the Son of God, died and rose from the dead to pay the price for your sinfulness and provide forgiveness.

Selah (Take your gear off for ten and pause and reflect.)

We have said previously that Jesus has already been seated at the right hand of the Father in the heavens. The seat at a ruler's right hand is a position of honor, authority, and a direct conduit of the ruler's sovereign power. (Read Matthew 26:64, Luke 22:69, and Acts 5:31.) In times past, the right side was referred to as the "dexter" and the left as the "sinister." It is quite possible this position of honor grew out of the fact that a majority of the weapon-carrying population wielded those weapons in their right hand. The king's most trusted combat leaders would fight on the right of their commander, protecting the hand and arm utilizing his weapon. Apparently it was quite an honor to be chosen to be to the right of your king. It's time to get moving again as Paul continues his thoughts; we read that His seat, which can be viewed as a sign of His authority, is:

1:21 Far Above Every Existing Authority

"Far above all principality, and power, and might, and dominion, and every name that is named, not only in this world, but also in that which is to come." (Eph. 1:21)

Jesus is far beyond all rule and authority, and He exercises power and dominion over every name that exists or ever will exist, and that definitely includes every commander or boss under whose authority you've ever served. Every king who has ever taken power, every president of every country, and every military commander-in-chief will also find themselves below Jesus in authority. He is called:

"The blessed and only Sovereign, the King of kings and Lord of lords every power is subject to Him." (1 Tim. 6:14–15)
"He is the head over all rule and authority; the rulers on this earth are subject to Him, even if they do not choose to glorify Him." (Col. 2:10)
"The king's heart is [like] channels of water in the hand of the LORD; He turns it wherever He wishes." (Prov. 21:1)

All through the Bible, you can read about rulers who did not serve God yet were often used to accomplish God's purpose. You may have heard about Caesar Augustus, a ruler of the old Roman Empire, who issued a seemingly strange order when he sent out a decree announcing that not only would the government be taxing its citizens and taking a census of them, but everyone would be required to travel to their city of origin to complete this task. This obligated a man named Joseph and his very pregnant fiancée, Mary, to travel to a town called Bethlehem, Joseph's hometown. God's Word had foretold that the Jewish Savior, the Messiah, would be born in Bethlehem, but with Mary and Joseph in Nazareth, Caesar's outwardly frivolous decree was just the thing to accomplish God's purpose. Though Caesar did not serve God, he served God's purpose.

On another occasion, God was about to pass judgment upon the Persian Empire. He desired that the faithful Jews be spared from the impending devastation. Since they were slaves of this evil empire, having been taken captive some seventy years prior, the Lord moved the heart of Cyrus, the King of Persia. Cyrus was supernaturally inspired to rebuild the temple in Jerusalem. He issued a public statement that was carried all over his kingdom, saying, "Any Jew is allowed to return to Israel and rebuild the temple, and I'll even compensate them for moving!" Once again, an ungodly ruler served His purpose.

This is so encouraging to me because I occasionally feel like I'm living in subjection to what is trying its darnedest to become a more and more godless form of government and an increasingly atheistic—or at least antagonistic—authority. Heaven knows, while our society and culture appear to have turned their heads away from God—some in shame and others because they have been attracted by the brilliance of the carnal world—nothing of this world can disrupt the plans of Our Lord. So I guess we really don't need to fear the decisions of our legislators, for the simple and biblical reason recorded in Colossians 1:16, "For by Him all things were created, [both] in the heavens and on earth, visible and invisible, whether thrones or dominions or rulers or authorities—all things have been created by Him and for Him." Each and every authority exists by God's ordination and is consciously or unconsciously working to accomplish God's ultimate plan and purpose. Since only God knows the plans He has for us, plans to give us a future and a hope, authorities will have little impact on those plans and should not cause us any concern.

In the rabbinic terms of the day, this verse also placed Christ above all orders of angels. (See Rom. 8:38; Eph. 3:10, 6:12; Col. 1:16, 2:10, 15; and Titus 3:11.)

This Age and the One to Come

I hope it has become obvious that Jesus' rule is not only over the authorities in this age but also in the ages to come. Some people are confused as to what is meant by "this age." When you read the Scriptures, you'll notice there are two separate ages, or periods of time, described in the Bible. Paul said that this present age is evil (Gal. 1:4). Jesus told us that at the end of the age, there would be a harvest (Matt. 13:39), that the angels will take out the wicked from among the righteous (Matt. 13:49), and that they will be burned with fire (Matt. 13:40). However, the age to come will commence with the resurrection of the dead (Luke 20:35), and Christians will receive eternal life (Mark 10:30,

Luke 18:30) and powers. This is always interesting to think about because we are so temporal in our thought processes. We act as though we believe the hypothesis that, as it says in 2 Peter 3:4, "all continues just as it was from the beginning of creation," but things haven't continued uninterrupted since creation. Until the day Noah entered the ark, people thought—just like you might now—that everything in life would always remain the same. Then things changed drastically. The earth as they knew it ceased to exist. Someday soon, the same will come to pass again, only this time the Bible tells us the earth won't be destroyed by water, but by fire. In 2 Peter 3:7–13, it says:

> The present heavens and earth by His word are being reserved for fire, kept for the Day of Judgment and destruction of ungodly men. But do not let this one [fact] escape your notice, beloved, that with the Lord one day is as a thousand years, and a thousand years as one day. The Lord is not slow about His promise, as some count slowness, but is patient toward you, not wishing for any to perish but for all to come to repentance. But the day of the Lord will come like a thief, in which the heavens will pass away with a roar and the elements will be destroyed with intense heat, and the earth and its works will be burned up. Since all these things are to be destroyed in this way, what sort of people ought you to be in holy conduct and godliness, looking for and hastening the coming of the day of God, on account of which the heavens will be destroyed by burning, and the elements will melt with intense heat! But according to His promise we are looking for new heavens and a new earth, in which righteousness dwells.

There are a lot of people thinking the new age begins with everyone receiving citizenship in the state of enlightenment. In reality, the new age will occur after the intellect of those folks has been enlightened by fire! This age is to end, and another age will begin. The age to come will have a new Heaven and a new earth. Jesus will be the Supreme Commander in that age as well.

1:22–23 Chief of the Church (COC)

"And hath put all [things] under His feet, and gave Him [to be] the head over all [things] to the church, which is His body, the fullness of Him that filleth all in all". (Eph. 1: 22–23)

The U.S. Navy has a position on submarines called Chief of the Boat, or COB for short. This Chief Petty Officer is, generally speaking, the most trusted and highest-ranking enlisted man on the submarine and is the commander's right-hand man (notice the vernacular reference to the position of honor again). It should not shock anyone that God the Father has made all things subject to His Son, Jesus Christ. Jesus is the go-to authority for all Christians, so it stands to reason that He would also be the authority over His Church. He certainly deserves to be, since He bought it, built it, and knows it inside and out. I realize this may be hard for you to understand, but Jesus is a Commander who voluntarily gave up His authority and in effect became an ordinary seaman. He then rose through the ranks to regain His position of absolute command, experiencing every thing a mortal man experiences along the way. My Lord and Savior is truly a "been there, done that and have the t-shirt and ball cap to prove it," do as I do, and not a "do as I say" leader. What more can you ask for?

The Church is often referred to as the Body of Christ because its members are the physical representation of Him on this earth. While He is in Heaven, we have been called to be His hands and His voice. When this call goes out, all too often these truths regarding Jesus's leadership are forgotten. Many congregations fail dismally in allowing Jesus to maintain His authority in His own Church. Instead, men decide how to run these churches. Many church leaders do not consider that as the Body of Christ we are individual ambassadors, called to do His will collectively, not our own. My desire in ministry is to do only what Christ would do, teach only what He would teach, and say only what He would say in all of my daily activities, an objective at which I often fall miserably short. As Paul said in 2 Corinthians 5:20, "We are ambassadors for Christ, as though God were entreating through us." This isn't just a leader's responsibility, but the responsibility of all of you who are in the Church. You are all called to serve in the Army of Christ and to be His voice, His hands, and His body. That means you must allow yourselves to be directed by the head, Jesus, and represent Him as perfectly as you can in this present, evil age.

Jesus said in John 9:5, "While I am in the world, I am the light of the world." Then He told us in Matthew 5:14–16:

> You are the light of the world. A city set on a hill cannot be hidden. Nor do [men] light a lamp, and put it under the peck-measure, but on the lampstand; and it gives light to all who are in the house. Let your light shine before men in such a way that they may see your good works, and glorify your Father who is in heaven.

You are His body on this earth, called to be His representative and His light in the world. You shouldn't need a WWJD (What Would Jesus Do) shirt, charm, or bracelet to remind you that even in the most difficult circumstances Jesus, the Head of the Church, would always DTRT (Do The Right Thing).

Selah (Take your gear off for ten and pause and reflect.)

As you look back over the first part of your journey through chapter one, you should see several key points more clearly. Key points Paul felt the Ephesians Christians, and you yourselves, should keep foremost in their minds and hearts, are that:

- Christ has blessed us in the heavenly places.
- He has chosen us before the foundation of the world.
- He has adopted us as sons.
- He has forgiven our sins.
- He promised us an inheritance.
- He sealed us with the Holy Spirit.
- He has made us His body.

2

If you are ready, troops, it's time to load up and head out as we begin looking into the wonders that await your investigation in chapter two. Paul is going to jog your memory and discuss with you of the state of your lives before you became Christians and received all of God's great blessings.

2:1–3 You Were Serving in the Wrong Army

> "And you [hath he quickened], who were dead in trespasses and sins; Wherein in time past ye walked according to the course of this world, according to the prince of the power of the air, the spirit that now worketh in the children of disobedience: Among whom also we all had our conversation in times past in the lusts of our flesh, fulfilling the desires of the flesh and of the mind; and were by nature the children of wrath, even as others." (Eph. 2:1–3)

As Christians, you must never forget that you were dead in the trespasses and sins in which you walked. I think this would be a good time to explain to you the difference between "trespasses" and "sins" as I understand it. I hope you'll find that my definitions are both valid and educational.

"Trespasses," as I understand the term, refers to the individual times that you blunder, the times when you deviate from the narrow path that leads to Heaven. It speaks of each incident of impropriety in which you've engaged.

"Sin," on the other hand, is derived from a word that means, "to miss the mark." In ancient Greek writings, the word was used to describe archers or spearmen who displayed a propensity for missing their anticipated targets. In modern terms, then, you might say to sin means "to miss the target."

A trespass refers to a single bad act you've committed, and sin is developing (notice I did not say cultivating—and there is a reason I didn't, which you will see later) and living a lifestyle that falls short of God's perfection. The Bible tells you in Romans 3:23, "All have sinned and fall short of the glory of God." So you see, not only you but all Christians and non-Christians alike have missed the bull's-eye of God's glorious perfection. In truth, we have often missed the entire target. Whether it's someone unashamedly heading into forbidden territory (we called it "Indian Country" in Vietnam), or whether it's someone who's trying to lead a good life on the path of righteousness but is detoured by sinful habits, everyone sins, is spiritually dead, and is separated from God until they are made alive through Christ. I guess that's why I believe that "bad" people, if the truth be told, can change, but only if they really want to and if they accept God's offered way to change.

The "Way" of the World

When people are spiritually dead, they are, in some ways, like the multitude of prisoners who are sitting on death row across our country, awaiting execution for their crimes against society. They might be referred to in prison vernacular as "dead men walking," though that term is really reserved for inmates on their last walk from their cell to the death chamber. When people choose to pursue the way of the world as so many do, following after the worldly examples that have been set before them, they are marching double-time toward a spiritual execution. The world says to go ahead and get drunk because it is fun, so they get drunk. Our society, if not the world, condones lying, and they convince themselves and others it is really OK to tell lies, especially if the end seems to justify the means. The world believes in seeking hedonistic forms of pleasure, and they become self-indulgent, no matter what the cost or who is hurt. The world is traveling down a six-lane highway to hell. God warns us that the road to perdition is wide and easily traveled, while the way to Heaven is narrow and no "rose garden." Notice God does not say the way is blocked or impassible, only difficult—a philosophy and an adjective that does not appeal to the nature of the carnal or natural man. But the azimuth that this world is determined to follow is contrary to God's ways and always has been.

In fact, this track is following the tactical plan prepared by "the prince of the power of the air," which is only one of the titles that the Bible uses for the Devil. Jesus labeled him "the ruler of this world" in John 14:30 and 16:11. It is easy to see why, because the world clamors after the Devil's example of sin and rebellion—against God as though it were the proverbial pot of gold at the end of the rainbow, which incidentally you should recall is a symbol of God's covenant not to once again flood the entire earth. Take heed, soldier, Satan is a master of disinformation and camouflage, and all you have to do is look around you. What appears as beauty and light is nothing but glittering "eye candy," and has no substance at all.

You Were a Child of Anger

If you are following the Devil's examples of living a self-centered lifestyle, you should expect to earn the same just reward the Devil earned—God's wrath. When you deliberately rebel against God and His standards, can you really expect to get away with that rebellion? Remember, God is still in control, even in the throes of chaos. So think logically about it for a moment and meditate on these next three examples.

- If God created sex exclusively for a permanent, heterosexual, monogamous marriage, then wouldn't it stand to reason that He would be livid with unmarried folks who elect to live together and have sex outside of marriage, or those who take pride in their sexual freedom and premarital or extramarital sexual conquests? Test-driving a heterosexual relationship was never a part of God's plan for your life. Remember, your vehicle and driver's licenses may have short-term expiration dates; your marriage license only expires when "death do you part."

- If God gave you skills and talents that were designed and intended for His glory, are you really surprised that it brings out His ire when you choose to use those talents to magnify your own pride and glory or, as He points out in the parable of the talents, you fail to use them at all?

- If God gave you something to be used for righteousness, wouldn't you expect Him to be upset if you used it for unrighteousness? Any logical man would. God does not use reverse psychology. When He says or does something, it may seem deep, but it is really very simple and straightforward. It is man who invented methods of making shallow things seem complex.

In the Bible, you read about a man named Balaam who had been gifted by God with an incredible ability to speak things and they would happen (Num. 22:6). God had granted Balaam this special ability to be used for righteousness. But when men came and offered him a lot of money to use this gift for unscrupulous purposes, he succumbed to the flattery and a chance to cash in on the opportunity. This made God angry enough to threaten to kill Balaam (Num. 22:33). A wise man once told me, "Flattery is like perfume, it is meant to be sniffed, not swallowed." Remember this saying. The point is, succumbing to flattery can be as deadly to a Christian as drinking a bottle of perfume. Keep reading and see what I mean.

Samson was another man God endowed with an amazing gift, a gift of remarkable physical strength. He was given this strength in order to deliver God's people from their enemies. But instead, Samson used his strength to follow his own agenda and plot his own course. For this reason Samson was judged and found wanting. For that he paid a price, but when you read the Scriptures regarding Samson, you will see that restoration is something God understands. He was never out of earshot during Samson's captivity.

God gifted Judas in the handling of money. But when he used his accounting skills to rip off the ministry and to betray Jesus so he could make more cash, he incurred the wrath of God and suffered the just consequences of his decisions. I think it is worth noting that there is both a similarity and a great difference between Peter and Judas. Both of them were unfaithful to Jesus. Judas betrayed Jesus for money, and Peter denied Him three times before the cock's crowing. Both felt enormous regret and shame. It seems that only Peter understood God's forgiveness, however. Peter lived and died for Christ while Judas lived and died for himself, despised his ill-gotten gain, and died for naught.

My friend, God has given every one of you gifts, talents, and skills, but many of you are choosing to use them for evil purposes or don't use them at all. And yet, when others try to lovingly communicate that you are a child of wrath, because you are following the Devil's example of disobedience, it doesn't seem to go over very well, does it? You see, God's wrath on rebellious and disobedient human beings isn't a popular dinner table topic, especially when it comes home to roost and can be deemed to have personal applications. There are not a lot of people who enjoy hearing what Jesus said in John 3:36, "He who does not obey the Son shall not see life, but the wrath of God abides on him." Fortunately, Jesus started that sentence by saying in John 3:36, "He who believes in the Son has eternal life," and that is the very good news. The one and only true God who hates trespasses, sin, disobedience, and rebellion happens to love you!

I think it is also important that I take a moment to remind you right here of a rather important and hopefully obvious point. You need to do more than read books like this one. In order to really understand the Bible, you need to read and study it. Topical books and commentaries will help, but nothing can substitute for your own direct knowledge of God's Word in its entirety. I say this because Satan and his warriors know more about the Bible than many Christians know. They also know how to use it out of context to devastate and lay waste to individuals and even corporate bodies. Imagine being told the following, all of which are truthful: "Judas went out and hung himself—go thou and do likewise—and what thou do, doest quickly." How would you respond? You need to know your arsenal inside out and know it well.

2:4–7 You Are Saved by God's Mercy and Love

"But God, who is rich in mercy, for his great love wherewith he loved us, Even when we were dead in sins, hath quickened us together with Christ, (by grace ye are saved;) And hath raised [us] up together, and made [us] sit together in heavenly [places] in Christ Jesus: That in the ages to come he might shew the exceeding riches of his grace in [his] kindness toward us through Christ Jesus." (Eph. 2:4–7)

Because of God's great love toward each of you personally, He has shown every one of you mercy. Mercy is the practice of not inflicting on people the punishment they deserve. It means that although someone should really be punished, that punishment is postponed or delayed. I truly believe God doesn't want to judge sinners and pour out His wrath on His own creation. The Bible tells us in 2 Peter 3:9 that God "is patient toward you, not wishing for any to perish but for all to come to repentance." So, God sits, waiting patiently, hating your sin but loving you, despising your rebellious nature and definitely wanting you to repent of it. He is obviously rich in mercy because He gives you opportunity after opportunity to turn away from your seemingly persistent rebellion and turn or "re-turn" to Him. But, He also tells us that when He returns, it will be like a thief in the night. This ought to provide evidence to even the most hardened of hearts that these opportunities are only available for a limited time and will not go on forever. No man knows when he will receive his last chance. Can you afford to keep watching and waiting? When you miss the rapture, there won't be another one coming along.

You Are Made Alive with Christ by Faith

When you begin to believe in Jesus Christ as your Lord and Savior, when that spark of faith begins to burn, it is like waking up from the dead. You were dead in trespasses and sins, and now you are becoming alive in Christ.

Faith—I mean real faith—is the thing that brings you from spiritual death to eternal life. You may be thinking, "I'd like to believe, but I'm from Missouri and sort of a skeptical person. I'm too intelligent to have faith in someone or something I can't see. So persuade me." Well, I am sorry, pal, but faith doesn't come by someone persuading you. The Bible tells you in Romans 10:17, "So faith [comes] from hearing, and hearing by the word of Christ." If you allow yourself to hear (and read, study, memorize, meditate on, and apply the teachings of) the Word of Christ, the Bible, you will find that you are going to develop an unconquerable faith with the help and guidance of the Holy Spirit. The Word of Christ will deliver you from death into life, and the Holy Spirit will be the Conviction, Comforter and Conscience of your transformed heart.

Let's take a moment to look at some transformations recorded in the Scriptures for a moment. In the Bible, you will find that Jesus raised three people from physical death.

One of these events took place when Jesus was walking into a city called Nain. He and his followers encountered a funeral procession leaving the city (Luke 7:12). The only son of a widow was being taken out for burial. Luke 7:14–15 says, "And He came up and touched the coffin; and the bearers came to a halt. And He said, 'Young man, I say to you, arise!' And the dead man sat up, and began to speak. And [Jesus] gave him back to his mother." With a single sentence, the Word of Christ brought that man from death into life.

Another instance occurred when Jesus' friend Lazarus got sick and died while Jesus was out of town. Everyone was terribly sad. Four days later, Jesus walked up to the tomb. The events are documented in John 11:43–44, "And when He had said these things, He cried out with a loud voice, 'Lazarus, come forth.' He who had died came forth." With a single sentence, another dead man came to life.

A third incident happened when a little twelve-year-old girl died. Her father begged Jesus to come to his house. "When Jesus walked in, He called, saying, 'Child, arise!' And her spirit returned, and she rose immediately" (Luke 8:54–55). Once more, the Word of Christ brought a dead person to life.

If He was able to accomplish these miraculous feats so easily, then can there be any doubt that He can just as easily resurrect your spiritual life? Let me point out that only because you and I tend to think so small do we require words like "miraculous" when God acts. From His point of view, there is nothing to it.

Showing His Grace

You may have begun today as a spiritual corpse: dead in trespasses and living a sinful way of life with nothing to anticipate but gloom, despair, and misery. You fully expect that God's wrath will one day come down upon you because of your callousness and rebelliousness. But now, as you continue learning about the Word of Christ, you may be gaining a little insight into faith. Perhaps you're starting to think, "I believe that just maybe God might love me—in spite of my sin! I believe that I'm beginning to come alive and see some light!"

Even though you might not be fully internalizing the biblical concepts written in this book, I'm going to stop here for a second and give you another opportunity to solidify your newly found faith. But before I do I'm going to ask you to bow your head and meditate on these words of Jesus in John 5:24–25:

> "Truly, truly, I say to you, he who hears My word, and believes Him who sent Me, has eternal life, and does not come into judgment, but has passed out of death into life. Truly, truly, I say to you, an hour is coming and now is, when the dead shall hear the voice of the Son of God; and those who hear shall live."

Have you heard the voice of Jesus Christ calling you from death to life? Remember, God says in Deuteronomy 30:19, "I have set before you life and death…So choose life in order that you may live." If you desire to choose life right now, and you desire to be a living manifestation of God's amazing grace, all you need to do is bow your head right where you are and admit to the Lord that you are a sinner lost in the world of sin and trespass. Acknowledge Him as the Son of God and your personal Savior and thank Him for saving you through His death on Calvary's Cross. Then read the book of Romans. Read it slowly and thoughtfully, followed by the book of John. When you begin to understand the how and the why of Christianity (or as close to understanding as you or I will ever get), you may then be ready to take on an in-depth study of books like James and Peter.

While you are studying these books, seek good counsel from older and wiser Christians. God has said the young shall learn from the old and though this does not always convert to age alone, older and wiser are not mutually exclusive terms either.

Selah (Take your gear off for ten and pause and reflect.)

OK, recruits, off your packs and off your backs, load 'em up, it's time to roll! The first seven verses of chapter two reminded us where we came from, dead in trespasses and sins. But because of God's love for us, He ransomed us and we no longer have to be dead men walking. We have been offered eternal life. Paul continues the thought now about how a loving God saved dead sinners like you and me.

2:8–9 Saved Only by Grace

"For by grace are ye saved through faith; and that not of yourselves: [it is] the gift of God: Not of works, lest any man should boast." (Eph. 2:8–9)

I have heard this passage of Scripture so many times in the last forty years that I often have to remind myself when I hear or read it, to be in awe of it. It is so basic, yet so deep; so easy to grasp, yet so difficult to accept; understandable in its simplicity, yet impossible in its complexity. It begins by pointing out that you're saved by grace. If you're saved by it, then grace must be an important concept to understand, wouldn't you agree? The word actually has a variety of meanings: kindness, favor, gift, and blessing. Most people who really understand grace have learned to refer to it as "undeserved favor." After analyzing passages like the following, it should become apparent to you that man has never at any time in recent history, nor does anyone living, now merit grace. This is a reiteration of what Paul has just said in verse five: "But God, being rich in mercy, because of His great love with which He loved us, even when we were dead in our transgressions, made us alive together with Christ (by grace you have been saved)" (Eph. 2:4–5). You were dead in transgressions (sinful lifestyles), but because of God's mercy, He gave you eternal life through Christ, saving you by His grace. This is unmerited favor indeed. You did nothing to deserve it; in fact you have often done quite the opposite. But thanks to God's love and mercy—an example of which you can read about in Romans 5:8, "God demonstrates His own love toward us, in that while we were yet sinners, Christ died for us"—you have been offered His saving grace. Paul could just as easily started this passage by saying, "For by God's blessing, kindness, gift, and favor (which none of you deserve), you have been saved."

What Do You Mean Saved?

"Saved" is another word that we sometimes fail to give a Christian definition to when we use it. Most people understand that it means to be rescued or delivered from danger, harm, or death. But when a Christian inquires about your salvation by saying,—"I'm saved. Are you saved? Do you want to be saved? Do you know how to get saved?"—what are they indicating that you need to be saved from? He or she may actually be referring to your being saved from many things. For example, when you're saved, the Bible tells us you have been "saved from this perverse generation" (Acts 2:40), and you are being saved from perishing in death (2 Thess. 2:10). Also, regarding the future, you shall be saved from the wrath of God (Rom. 5:9), whose wrath will ultimately come upon the earth and all the unsaved who occupy it. There is also an eternal judgment that you are saved from (Heb. 5:9). With that in mind, maybe now you can understand this passage of Scripture: "For by God's blessing, kindness, gift, and favor (which you didn't deserve), you have been saved from this corrupt world, from death, from wrath, and from eternal judgment."

So Do You Know What Faith Really Is?

Next, we will see that salvation happens through faith. Of course, faith is simply defined as a belief that is acted on. But not just any kind of faith activates God's grace. After all, some people have enough faith in their favorite teams to bet money on the outcome of their games. Others have enough faith to pay a parcel or freight courier to absolutely, positively get their package delivered overnight and expect it to arrive on time. Still others have enough faith in the aeronautical engineers who are working for the various aircraft manufacturers like McDonnell Douglas or Lockheed-Martin to book their airline travel with complete confidence that they will arrive at their destination safely. But the Bible is much more specific about exactly what kind of faith will save us by grace. Acts 20:21 explains that it is "faith in our Lord Jesus Christ." Jesus said that people "have been sanctified by faith in Me" (Acts 26:18). Paul said in

Galatians 2:20, "I live by faith in the Son of God." A saving faith is faith in Jesus Christ and only Him. (Also take a look at Acts 3:16, 24:24; Rom. 3:22, 3:26; James 2:1; and Rev. 14:12.) Regardless of what may be politically correct, a sincere belief in some other religion or person is a genuinely wrong belief and will not save anyone. The Bible teaches that "God has chosen you from the beginning for salvation through sanctification by the Spirit and faith in the truth" (2 Thess. 2:13). It is only faith in Jesus Christ that saves. No amount of faith in a lie will save anyone. But it's not just believing in something. Faith must be active and not merely pro forma.

I heard a story once that puts an earthly perspective on faith as it relates to belief. It goes like this: A man once came to Niagara Falls, New York, intending to walk a tightrope across the falls. A great deal of publicity was generated, and on the day he was to perform, the shorelines of both sides of the falls were lined with onlookers. When it was time to walk, one unremarkable man came forth from the crowd and picking up a balance pole, began to walk across the cable stretched between the USA and Canada. He walked rapidly across, to the astonishment of many who had not really believed the event would ever take place. After crossing the falls, the man began his trip back across and, at about the halfway mark, he stopped and threw away his balance pole and continued to walk across without it. The crowd roared with approval. The man then went out on the cable and began to do a series of tricks that included handstands, summersaults, hops, and other acrobatic feats. The crowd was enthralled and awestruck with the man's abilities. After riding a bicycle across, stopping the bike, balancing on the handlebars, and standing on the seat, the man came back to the end of the cable and picked up a wheelbarrow, which he promptly placed on the cable. He then turned and spoke to the enthusiastic crowd for the first time. He said, "Who believes that I can walk across this cable pushing this wheelbarrow?" The impressed crowd overwhelmingly indicated their belief. He then asked, "How many of you believe I can do it blindfolded?" Again there were a great many believers in the crowd. The man then pointed to a man in the crowd who had vehemently indicated his belief and politely said, "Please, get in the wheelbarrow." That, my friends, is when belief becomes faith or, as I have heard it said, it is "where the rubber meets the road."

So if we continue the paraphrasing of this verse, we can now say, "For by God's blessing, kindness, gift, and favor (which you didn't deserve), you have been saved from this corrupt world, from death, from wrath, and from judgment by your active belief in the truth of Jesus Christ."

The Gift of God

Now before some of you troopers begin complaining and say it isn't fair that only people with faith in Jesus get to be saved, it is important to note that once again God didn't shortchange anyone. He prepared us all at birth with a foundation of faith, as we are told in Romans 12:3, "God has allotted to each a measure of faith." "Every human being is born with some faith residing within their heart, so everyone is without excuse" (Rom. 1:20). Jesus Christ not only placed that faith inside of us at birth, He wants that faith to grow and reach completion. That is why Jesus is called in Hebrews 12:2, "the author and perfector of faith." With that perspective in mind, let's look once more at the paraphrase.

"For by God's blessing, kindness, gift, and favor (which you didn't deserve), you have been saved from this corrupt world, from death, from wrath, and from judgment by your active belief in the truth of Jesus Christ, Who, by the way, put that belief in your heart in the first place."

Not as a Result of Works

No one I ever knew or heard of has ever been saved by religious works. No matter how much money you donate, no matter how many hours of your life you spend in church, no matter how many good deeds you do, no matter how many prayers you say, you will be no closer to Heaven than a murderer on death row unless you get saved by grace through faith in your Savior, Jesus Christ. The Bible tells you flat out in 2 Timothy 1:9 that God "has saved us, and called us with a holy calling, not according to our works, but according to His own purpose and grace which was granted us in Christ Jesus." Troops, this is one of the biggest ambushes Satan sets up, and you must avoid it at all costs. It is sprung on unsuspecting Christians who sometimes begin—after hearing too many feel-good sermons—to think their religious works can save them. Others who aren't Christians yet are led by Satan and his followers to believe that very good people can easily get into Heaven just by being nice, kind, and by doing things for others. This may sound harmless, but it is not! For nowhere in that philosophy do you find God. But if you go back, you'll remember that it is God's grace that saves you, not your works (lest any man should boast—something we humans, and men especially, do all too well). It is God's goodness and His grace, not yours, that provides for your redemption. We Marines know no one can award themselves the title of U.S. Marine. It must be awarded to you, but only after you have met all the requirements.

Salvation also must be awarded, but again only after you have satisfied all of the requirements God has decreed: none are dependent on your works.

Selah (Take your gear off for ten and pause and reflect.)

Has Paul made his point clear enough for you yet? The first point is that you were dead in your sins but made alive in Christ. The second is that, after you have been given this new life, you recognize that your one purpose in life is to do the good works of God, the opportunities for which He prepares for each of us in advance and expects us to accomplish. I hope so, because now he is going to point out, well, you might as well grab your gear and get back in the war.

2:10–12 The Transition from Gentile Civilian to Christian Soldier Begins

"For we are his workmanship, created in Christ Jesus unto good works, which God hath before ordained that we should walk in them. Wherefore remember, that ye [being] in time past Gentiles in the flesh, who are called Uncircumcision by that which is called the Circumcision in the flesh made by hands; That at that time ye were without Christ, being aliens from the commonwealth of Israel, and strangers from the covenants of promise, having no hope, and without God in the world." (Eph. 2:10–12)

When Jesus walked the earth, and for quite some time thereafter, the Jews held no love for anyone who was not a Jew. They grouped every non-Jew into the category of Gentiles. They called them, among other derogatory words, "uncircumcised." Jewish laws even mandated this prejudice. In Acts 10, Peter discussed the situation with a crowd of Gentiles at Cornelius' house. Acts 10:28 says, "You yourselves know how unlawful it is for a man who is a Jew to associate with a foreigner or to visit him." And later, Peter got in big trouble with the Jews for this visit to a Gentile's home. Acts 11:2–3 says, "And when Peter came up to Jerusalem, those who were circumcised took issue with him, saying, 'You went to uncircumcised men and ate with them.'"

It is evident that the Jews hated the Gentiles. But to say that they merely hated them would be a masterful understatement. Hate is too delicate a declaration. In reality, they violently despised them. You can see an example of this seething hatred documented in Luke 4. Jesus was preaching in His hometown synagogue in Nazareth. You will find that He was reading the Scriptures and teaching with authority, and all who heard were amazed and impressed. Luke 4:22 says, "And all were speaking well of Him, and wondering at the gracious words that were falling from His lips." But then His sermon took an unantici-pated detour. He said, in Luke 4:25–27:

> "But I say to you in truth, there were many widows in Israel in the days of Elijah, when the sky was shut up for three years and six months, when a great famine came over all the land; and yet Elijah was sent to none of them, but only to Sarepta, [in the land] of Sidon, to a woman who was a widow. And there were many lepers in Israel in the time of Elisha the prophet; and none of them was cleansed, but only Naaman the Syrian."

Those of you reading this who are not familiar with the Scriptures may miss what Jesus was saying. He deliberately mentioned these two stories from the Old Testament—the widow of Zarephath in Sidon, who was miraculously ministered to by Elijah in 1 Kings 17, and Naaman the Syrian, who was cleansed from leprosy in 2 Kings 5—because both of these people were Gen-tiles, and Jesus was making a point of saying that although there were many Jews around, God intentionally ministered to these people instead.

Those people listening to Jesus' sermon did not miss His point. Luke 4:28–29 says, "And all in the synagogue were filled with rage as they heard these things; and they rose up and cast Him out of the city, and led Him to the brow of the hill on which their city had been built, in order to throw Him down the cliff." Not surprisingly, this was not an isolated incident. In Acts 22, Paul was explaining his ministry to a massive crowd in the temple. He writes of God calling him, "And He said to me, 'Go! For I will send you far away to the Gentiles.' And they listened to him up to this statement, and [then] they raised their voices and said, 'Away with such a fellow from the earth, for he should not be allowed to live!'" (Acts 22:21–22). You have seen here just how much the Jews hated the Gentiles, so much that they would not associate, visit, or even eat with them. When anyone suggested to them that God would actually minister to the Gentiles, they would become enraged—even to the point of murder.

Gentile Hopelessness without God

The people in Ephesus were Gentiles. Hated by the Jews, having no covenant with God, and not yet really knowing Jesus Christ, their situation was desperate, or as Paul describes it in Ephesians 2:12, "Having no hope and without God in the world." That sounds a lot like your plight and mine, doesn't it? No hope without God.

I used to hear guys getting ready to fight say, "There ain't nothing separating us but fear and air. You eliminate one, and I'll eliminate the other." That sounds like it takes two people to get the job done. Your salvation also takes two parties doing their part: you and God. He's done His part, now how about you doing yours? Repent right now and be revived for eternity. You are saved by grace, through faith plus nothing!

2:13–18 Brought Near by the Blood of Christ

> "But now in Christ Jesus, ye who sometimes were far off are made nigh by the blood of Christ. For he is our peace, who hath made both one, and hath broken down the middle wall of partition [between us]; Having abolished in his flesh the enmity, [even] the law of commandments [contained] in ordinances; for to make in himself of twain one new man, [so] making peace; And that he might reconcile both unto God in one body by the Cross, having slain the enmity thereby: And came and preached peace to you which were afar off, and to them that were nigh. For through him we both have access by one Spirit unto the Father". (Eph. 2:13–18)

The Jews and Gentiles were, in biblical times, alienated from each other by extreme hate and bitterness on both sides. Here Paul teaches us that in Christ the rift exists no more; the dividing wall of enmity has been destroyed forever. Yes, it was knocked down, thus illuminating the way to Heaven for both Jew and Gentile. Through the Cross both have been made as one. Through Jesus, mankind is no longer divided into Gentiles or Jews. You who follow the teachings of the Bible are simply called Christians. There is one body in the His Church, and Christ is the head. Just like Paul told the Galatians in Galatians 3:28, "There is neither Jew nor Greek, there is neither slave nor free man, there is neither male nor female; for you are all one in Christ Jesus."

As Christians, we're all on a level playing field, and there should be no animosity between us.

Eradicating Hostility and Proliferating Peace

In light of what we just discussed, I am going to pose what may seem like some difficult questions for every Christian. Be honest when you answer the following questions. Can you honestly say about every Christian you know that there is no division, no enmity? Can you say that you are at peace with them, reconciled to them, and that you are one with each other? The sad truth is that most Christians cannot answer yes to all of these questions with integrity. Most of you know a person who as you might say, "lights your fire," even when you merely think about them. Most of you also know someone who you try to avoid when you see them, even from across the parking lot. Some of you begin to get angry at the mention of certain people's names. I'm not trying to beat you up, but I'm going to be brutally honest with you: this is just not acceptable to God. It is a trespass against Him and a symptom of a potentially sinful lifestyle. Whether it is bitterness, unforgiveness, or anger that you embrace, it is still immoral. It chokes out your fruitfulness, keeps you from growing, and hinders your prayers. At the Cross, Jesus abolished your differences. He made you all one body, and He preached peace. Yet you tell Him you don't want to be in the same state as someone; you don't want to be in the same neighborhood as someone; you don't want to circulate in the same social circles as someone; you don't even want to attend the same church as someone. It says in Ephesians 2:18 that in order to reach the Father, you must be in the same Spirit with Him, "For through Him we both have our access in one Spirit to the Father." Does what I just described sound like the embodiment of the Spirit of God to you? If it makes any difference to you, these questions are no easier for me to answer than they are for you and many other Christians, church leaders, or non-believers. We all need to heed Paul's wise counsel and crucify our natural and sinful nature every day of our lives and ask the Holy Spirit to complete His mission in us and help us to overcome our prejudicial feelings and man-made barriers.

2:19–22 Fellow Citizen Soldiers of Christ

"Now therefore ye are no more strangers and foreigners, but fellow citizens with the saints, and of the household of God; And are built upon the foundation of the apostles and prophets, Jesus Christ himself being the chief corner [stone]; In whom all the building fitly framed together groweth unto an holy temple in the Lord: In whom ye also are builded together for an habitation of God through the Spirit." (Eph. 2:19–22)

Every born-again Christian in the world is a citizen of Heaven and fellow laborer with every other Christian. We are all part of the same body, the Body of Christ, and we worship in the same house, the House of God. We all walk on the same foundation provided by the Word of God, with Christ as the cornerstone of that foundation. You are all one and in One. Therefore you must not allow yourselves to be divided. Jesus said in Matthew 12:25, "Any kingdom divided against itself is laid waste; and any city or house divided against itself shall not stand." When the house of God is divided, it becomes powerless. That's why Paul admonished the Corinthians in 1 Corinthians 1:10–11, "Now I exhort you, brethren, by the name of our Lord Jesus Christ, that you all agree, and there be no divisions among you, but you be made complete in the same mind and in the same judgment. For I have been informed concerning you, my brethren, by Chloe's [people,] that there are quarrels among you." If you're not in unity, you're not complete. He also told the Philippian Church in Philippians 4:2–3, "I urge Euodias, and I urge Syntyche to live in harmony in the Lord. Indeed, true comrade, I ask you also to help these women who have shared my struggle in [the cause of] the gospel, together with Clement also, and the rest of my fellow workers, whose names are in the book of life."

If you experience difficulty with someone who is a Christian, remind yourself that his or her name is also written in the book of life. Make a point to strive daily to maintain unity and harmony and keep the Church undivided. Meditate on these words from Hebrews 12 and let them minister to your heart as you deliberate on this passage of Scripture from Hebrews: 12:14–15 "Pursue peace with all men, and the sanctification without which no one will see the Lord. See to it that no one comes short of the grace of God; that no root of bitterness springing up causes trouble, and by it many be defiled".

Selah (Take your gear off for ten and pause and reflect.)

As we wrap up chapter two of the book of Ephesians, you have either learned for the first time, or have been reminded that the Jews and the Gentiles have been made one in Christ. Upon becoming Christians, these two foes that formerly hated one another were unified. Paul is now about to spend a great deal of chapter three pointing out that his ministry is directed (by God, if you recall) toward the Gentiles. Like he does in all of his writings, Paul will provide you with a lot of information. There are still many things to learn; so look smart, step lively, and let's get cookin', shall we?

3

3:1–3 The Prisoner of Christ Jesus

"For this reason I, Paul, the prisoner of Christ Jesus for the sake of you Gentiles—if indeed you have heard of the stewardship of God's grace which was given to me for you; that by revelation there was made known to me the mystery, as I wrote before in brief". (Eph. 3:1–3)

Paul really was a prisoner. He was in the custody of the Roman government. He did not, however, consider himself a prisoner of Rome. He considered himself instead a prisoner to the will of Christ Jesus. He wasn't just a prisoner incarcerated in a jail for the sake of Jesus. He acknowledged that he was also a prisoner because he was bound to the will of Jesus. You see, Paul described the Christian life in Romans 6:22 as "having been freed from sin and enslaved to God." A bondservant of God's, subject to God's will and to His plan for your lives, not your own. Paul lived his life after his conversion experience in the shadow of this form of slavery, entirely submissive to God's will rather than his own, even as it applied to his ministry. You may not remember, but Paul's real passion and earnest desire was not to be the apostle to the Gentiles. He fervently wanted to be a messenger of the Gospel to his own people, the Jews. Just read through the book of Acts, and you'll find that this was Paul's heartfelt mission. He even wrote about it in his letter to the Romans, "I have great sorrow and unceasing grief in my heart. For I could wish that I myself were accursed, [separated] from Christ for the sake of my brethren, my kinsmen according to the flesh, who are Israelites" (Rom. 9:2–4). In Romans 10:1 he says, "Brethren, my heart's desire and my prayer to God for them is for [their] salvation."

Yes, Paul wanted to be a minister to the Jews, but God allowed him no success in that venue. In accordance with His own will, He sent Paul as His ambassador to the Gentiles. Paul had very little ministry among the Jews. Today, though, his epistles frequently incite the transformed hearts of the Messianic Jews. God's plans were different than Paul's, just as God's plans frequently differ from our own. It is just as He declared through the prophet Isaiah in Isaiah 55:8–9, "'For My thoughts are not your thoughts, neither are your ways My ways,' declares the LORD. 'For [as] the heavens are higher than the earth, so are My ways higher than your ways, and My thoughts than your thoughts.'"

You see, my friends, God had a course charted for each of your lives even before you existed, and very often it is not the same course you might choose. Following God's plan is one of the most difficult tests you will face as a Christian. It is a test that measures whether you've truly given your life to Christ, or whether you're just trying to exploit God as a source of power and blessing you feel you can use to realize your own personal desires. When your will collides with God's will, there will always be a battle to see if you will be among those who fall back on your training and utter the prayer Christ uttered in Luke 22:42, "Yet not my will, but Thine be done." All good leaders realize that before you can truly lead anyone, you need to learn to follow wisely. In the Corps, we call that trait, when it is displayed, "followership." God has called on and is calling on Christians to help lead others out of the darkness and into the light. Have you learned a sufficient amount about following God's instructions to assume the leadership assignment He has you destined to fill?

3:4–7 A Mystery Exposed

> "By referring to this, when you read you can understand my insight into the mystery of Christ, which in other generations was not made known to the sons of men, as it has now been revealed to His holy apostles and prophets in the Spirit; to be specific, that the Gentiles are fellow heirs and fellow members of the body, and fellow partakers of the promise in Christ Jesus through the gospel, of which I was made a minister, according to the gift of God's grace which was given to me according to the working of His power." (Eph. 3:4–7)

Paul uses the word "mystery" in Ephesians more than in any other book of the Bible. Pronounced "*Moos-TAY-ree-on*" in the Greek, it refers to something that is hidden or secret. Jesus told His disciples that there were indeed mysteries in the kingdom of God, but that it has been arranged for us to know some of them (Matt. 13:11; Mark 4:11; Luke 8:10). Paul told the Corinthians that Christians are "stewards of the mysteries of God" (1 Cor. 4:1). Some of the mysteries that have been revealed to us are mysteries regarding such events as the rapture (1 Cor. 15:51), the typological picture of Christ and the Church that marriage represents (Eph. 5:32), and God's will (Eph. 1:9).

In this case, the mystery Paul is talking about is that the Gentiles are fellow heirs to the inheritance, fellow members of the body, and fellow partakers of the promise. They are just as eligible to be saved through Jesus Christ as the Jews are. This might not sound like an earth-shattering revelation to you today, but that's because you're used to dealing with the equality idea, at least as a society. To the Jews and Gentiles of Paul's day, however, this disclosure was as amazing and unconventional a teaching as the theory of space exploration.

3:8–10 Rank and Privileges

"To me, the very least of all saints, this grace was given, to preach to the Gentiles the unfathomable riches of Christ, and to bring to light what is the administration of the mystery which for ages has been hidden in God who created all things; so that the manifold wisdom of God might now be made known through the church to the rulers and the authorities in the heavenly places". (Eph. 3:8–10)

Paul recognized that his assigned ministry was completely undeserved. He knew it was conferred upon him only through God's grace. Even when writing to the Corinthians, he spoke humbly of himself, saying in 1 Corinthians 15:9, "I am the least of the apostles." Now we find him saying that he is the least of the saints. He proclaims without an iota of shame that he is a servant to every Christian in the Church. This kind of honest humility among leaders and preachers, especially in Western culture, is rarely observed today, but it is still absolutely necessary. Whenever I'm tempted to get a bit full of myself thinking, "I'm a leader, I'm in charge, I'm Ray, I'm a big shot. I know exactly what needs to be done and just how to do it," God just "rings my bell" and puts my whole life and ministry back into perspective by reminding me of what Paul told the Corinthians in 1 Corinthians 1:26–29:

"For consider your calling, brethren, that there were not many wise according to the flesh, not many mighty, not many noble; but God has chosen the foolish things of the world to shame the wise, and God has chosen the weak things of the world to shame the things which are strong, and the base things of the world and the despised, God has chosen, the things that are not, that He might nullify the things that are, that no man should boast before God."

It is wise to remember that touting our humility smacks of pride. It might behoove us to remember that when God chose the weak and foolish, He was choosing us. When I start thinking I'm somebody special, I feel ashamed and chastised. And well I should, for if I'm truly one of those He's called, it is only because I was incompetent, foolish, weak, and despised. Paul knew that his ministry (and everyone else's) was only bestowed by God's grace. With that in mind, I fully expect to be learning from you someday soon.

The Church Passes in Review for the Heavenlies

Another thing Paul points out in these verses seems incredible. For ages, the Gospel was predominantly concealed from angels and demons in the spiritual realm. But now the Church is allowed to reveal it to them! Do you recall when Peter said in 1 Peter 1:12, "These things which now have been announced to you through those who preached the gospel to you by the Holy Spirit sent from heaven—things into which angels long to look." The angels who longed to look into these things are now watching the Church on earth (as intently as some of us watch the soaps) to learn about them. That fact alone is so profoundly amazing! But, even beyond interesting, it is critical that you remember that the spirits are watching you all the time. Jesus said in Luke 15:10, "I tell you, there is joy in the presence of the angels of God over one sinner who repents." Paul said to Timothy, "I solemnly charge you in the presence of God and of Christ Jesus and of [His] chosen angels, to maintain these principles" (1 Tim. 5:21). And to the Corinthians he said, "For, I think, God has exhibited us apostles last of all, as men condemned to death; because we have become a spectacle to the world, both to angels and to men" (1 Cor. 4:9). They're watching when you sin and when you repent. They're watching the way you live and the way you die. Sort of makes you want to stop and think about straightening up your act a bit, doesn't it? Even when you are sure nobody can possibly see, know, or find out whatever it is you do not want revealed, you should now clearly see how futile that desire for secrecy really is. Your performance is always under critique, not only by non-Christians, but also by the residents of Heaven.

3:11–13 Developing Boldness and Confident Access

"This was in accordance with the eternal purpose which He carried out in Christ Jesus our Lord, in whom we have boldness and confident access through faith in Him. Therefore I ask you not to lose heart at my tribulations on your behalf, for they are your glory." (Eph. 3:11–13)

Thus far in chapter three you should have learned at least four things. Let's test your acuity, here they are:

1.   God will test us to see if we are truly willing to be enslaved to Him: His will versus our will.

2.   Why He really has selected us for salvation has been a mystery to most of mankind for hundreds of years.

3.   He desires to use us in ministry, not because of our greatness, but because we are anything but great and mighty.

4.   The angels—both good and bad (the bad ones are often referred to as demons)—are watching us all the time to see whether we will give in to sin or try our hardest to remain holy.

How much did you remember? All these things seem to follow a common thread leading to this culminating conclusion: in Jesus you can have boldness and confident access to the Throne of God, through faith in Him. Have you been avoiding the throne of God because you've been marching to the world's—or your own—cadence? Don't you understand that you've been offered salvation in spite of your dishonor? That God knew you were nothing when He called you? Do you now grasp the fact that your actions and those of other Christians are educating not only others, but even the angels themselves to the wonder of God's grace? Yes, it is still all about grace. The grace you couldn't and didn't earn. The grace He freely offered you. So for you to feel defeated and afraid to approach God is ridiculous. It is not a sign of the leadership God wants you to acquire. Never forget it is only because of your simple but firm faith in Jesus that you can approach the throne. Hebrews 4:16 says, "Let us therefore draw near with confidence to the throne of grace, that we may receive mercy and may find grace to help in time of need."

Selah (Ground your gear, take time to pause and reflect.)

You should readily understand by now that God called Paul as an apostle to the Gentiles in order that he might make clear to them that they were also fellow heirs to the heavenly inheritance, fellow members of the Body of Christ, and fellow partakers of the promise. The Army of God now has a whole new population from which to recruit. Now Paul says, "For this reason," or "Because of this." So if you are as curious as I am, bugler sound "Boots and Saddles" and let's see what he is about to undertake for the Lord.

3:14–16 Paul's Responsibility and Goals for Us

> "For this reason I bow my knees before the Father, from whom every family in heaven and on earth derives its name, that He would grant you, according to the riches of His glory, to be strengthened with power through His Spirit in the inner man…" (Eph. 3:14–16)

Paul was the primary person who'd brought the Gospel to the Gentiles during the early church years, and because of this he felt a strong sense of responsibility when it came to praying for their spiritual growth, maturity, and development. He was praying here specifically for them to be strengthened with power through God's Spirit. The power of the Holy Spirit is something that has been the subject of a great deal of misunderstanding and has even caused fear among some Christians. If you can manage to get rid of your preconceptions, misinformation, and convenient dogma and overcome your fear and trepidation, then you can look biblically and objectively at the person of the Holy Spirit.

The Bible plainly reveals to you that the source of power in any believer's life is the Holy Spirit. Because that power is biblical, it is not anything to be afraid of or embarrassed about. The prophet Micah told you in Micah 3:8, "I am filled with power—With the Spirit of the LORD," and Jesus, you realize, walked in the power of the Spirit (Luke 4:14) and promised the same thing to the disciples, "You shall receive power when the Holy Spirit has come upon you; and you shall be My witnesses both in Jerusalem, and in all Judea and Samaria, and even to the remotest part of the earth" (Acts 1:8). The Holy Spirit's power can come upon you and fill you—and does fill the life of a true Christian soldier. This power can manifest itself in either physical or spiritual ways. Physically it is evidenced through Mary, because we know that she was a virgin when Christ was conceived in her womb through the power of the Spirit. The angel Gabriel told her, "The Holy Spirit will come upon you, and the power of the Most High will overshadow you; and for that reason the holy offspring shall be called the Son of God" (Luke 1:35). Jesus, too, provided additional physical evidence of the power of the Spirit when He healed people. Acts 10:38 says, "God anointed Him with the Holy Spirit and with power, and He went about doing good, and healing all who were oppressed by the Devil." Paul also told the Romans that Christ had accomplished visible signs and wonders through him "in the power of the Spirit" (Rom 15:19).

It is unmistakably clear that the power of the Spirit can accomplish miraculous things physically. But the power of the Spirit can be verified as working inwardly as well. Seemingly invisible, the power of the Holy Spirit performs miracles inside of us as well. I am a sinner, as corrupt and carnal as any of you. But God continues to change me inwardly through the power of the Spirit. And brother, that is nothing short of miraculous! Even though I am bombarded daily by temptation, the Lord gives me the strength to resist sin through the power of His Spirit. That is the supernatural help I need! I may still get discouraged occasionally and tumble into doubt, but through the power of the Spirit, He instills hope in my heart (Rom. 15:13). The power of the Spirit does these miraculous things inside of each Christian, and that's what Paul was praying for, that they would be strengthened "in the inner man."

Paul's prayer is also my prayer for everyone who acknowledges Christ as his or her Savior. The outcome of that supernatural strengthening is so important to each and every one of you. Paul tells you what that outcome is supposed to be in the next three verses.

3:17–19 The Result of Being Strengthened with Power

"...so that Christ may dwell in your hearts through faith; and that you, being rooted and grounded in love, may be able to comprehend with all the saints what is the breadth and length and height and depth, and to know the love of Christ which surpasses knowledge, that you may be filled up to all the fullness of God". Eph. 3:17–19)

Paul is praying for the Ephesians to be strengthened with the Spirit's power so that three things will happen.

1. He prays that Christ will dwell in their hearts through faith.

2. He prays that they will be able to comprehend the unfathomable love of Christ.

3. He prays that they may be filled up with all the fullness of God

Christ's Indwelling

We know that when someone becomes a Christian, Jesus comes into his or her life and heart. Still, Paul asks the Corinthians, "Do you not recognize this about yourselves, that Jesus Christ is in you?" (2 Cor. 13:5). Even the Gentile Colossians had to be reminded that Christ was in them (Col. 1:27). Paul's statement might confuse some of you who think, "If Christ is already in me, then why do I need to be strengthened with the power of the Spirit for Christ to dwell in my heart?" The explanation, though not obvious in English, is fairly clear in the Greek. The Greek word used is pronounced '*kat-oy-KEH-o*', which is here translated "to dwell," and literally means "to be completely at home." It is an unfortunate but true statement that, while many Christians have invited Christ into their hearts to be their Savior, they just can't seem to let Him feel at home. They often act like an unpaid landlord and keep locking Him out. I know you have heard this preached many times. Jesus says in Revelation 3:20, "Behold, I stand at the door and knock; if anyone hears My voice and opens the door, I will come in to him, and will dine with him, and he with Me." It is even quoted frequently as an evangelistic invitation, and yet Jesus directed this Scripture to those Christians in the Church of Laodicea, the church that, if you remember, was allegedly Christian yet needed to repent for their lukewarm walk! Are you truly strengthened by the power of the Holy Spirit? Was the first result of the Lord coming to live in your heart your complete abdication, to the point that Jesus became completely at home, settling in like it really was His own home?

Grasping the Love of Christ

When you are strengthened by the power of the Spirit, you become rooted and grounded in love, which enables you to begin to comprehend the immeasurable love of Christ. How can any person possibly know something that surpasses knowledge? It seems impossible, doesn't it? Yet when you are strengthened by the power of the Spirit, your knowledge of God's love begins to expand. The more grounded you are in love, the more knowledge you gain of the love of Christ. Only through the power of the Spirit can we sacrificially love others and learn more about the love of God. Then and only then, can your understanding increase, and the Scriptures that speak about God's love for you open up and take on an even deeper meaning. One of the first Scriptures most people hear is John 3:16. It is so often quoted that most people think it is too basic a thought to meditate on. But listen to it carefully, "For God so loved the world, that He gave His only begotten Son, that whoever believes in Him should not perish, but have eternal life." It says God loved the world—our corrupt and often contemptuous world—enough to sacrifice His Son (His only Son) even unto death, for a world that had turned its back on Him time after time. Every time I consider that, its significance to me increases. It signifies an even more intense love than I could have imagined before I became a Christian. If I wasn't being strengthened by the power of the Spirit, I certainly wouldn't be growing in love, and I would probably just be saying, "Yup, John 3:16. Been there, heard it before, and got the T-shirt in my bottom drawer."

Filled up to all the Fullness of God

Paul had an intense desire for the Ephesians (and you) to be filled up with all the fullness of God. How can I even begin to explain to you what the fullness of God is? Why don't I just let you think and talk about the following things God says about it.

> "May grace and peace be yours in fullest measure." (1 Pet. 1:2)
> "Fill you with all joy and peace" (Rom. 15:13)
> "Filled with the Spirit" (Eph. 5:18)
> "Filled with the fruit of righteousness"(Phil. 1:11)
> "With full conviction" (1 Thess. 1:5)
> "Filled with the knowledge of His will" (Col. 1:9)

"Fully assured" (Col. 4:12)

"Fully supplying the needs of the saints" (2 Cor. 9:12)

The list could go on forever! Do you have a desire to be strengthened with power through God's Spirit? Many people think of this as an unattainable or impossible desire. They say, "God would never give me all that, because I can never be that strong of Christian."

But, with a little joy in your heart, take a look at the very next verse......

3:20–21 Beyond all our Expectations

"Now to Him who is able to do far more abundantly beyond all that we ask or think, according to the power that works within us, to Him be the glory in the church and in Christ Jesus to all generations forever and ever. Amen". (Eph. 3:20–21)

God is ready, willing, and able to do exceedingly and abundantly far beyond all that you could ever ask or think. Do you desire to be strengthened by the power of the Holy Spirit today? Listen to what Jesus said in Luke 11:9–13:

I say to you, ask, and it shall be given to you; seek, and you shall find; knock, and it shall be opened to you. For everyone who asks, receives; and he who seeks, finds; and to him who knocks, it shall be opened. Now suppose one of you fathers is asked by his son for a fish; he will not give him a snake instead of a fish, will he? Or [if] he is asked for an egg, he will not give him a scorpion, will he? If you then, being evil, know how to give good gifts to your children, how much more shall [your] heavenly Father give the Holy Spirit to those who ask Him?

If you desire or need the work of the Holy Spirit in your life today, all you have to do is ask God to work in your life. He will always help you because He is a loving Father.

Selah (Ground your gear, take time to pause and reflect.)

We are about to come to another verse in our study of the book of Ephesians that begins with the word "therefore." While some of you may tire of hearing the old Bible study rule that goes like this, "When you see a 'therefore,' it means that we need to stop and find out what it's 'there for.'" The word is, as always, an indicator that you must go back and review what has previously been said. Since the idea you're about to be introduced to builds on the foundation of what you have just covered, you need only go back one verse and remind yourselves that Paul has just said God must be always be given glory in the Church. Thus, this "therefore" means, "Because God is to be given glory in the Church..." All right, trooper, enough of this lollygagging, stand by for orders.

You have reached a point in your training where you ought to be able to talk the talk of a follower of Christ, but can you walk the painful way of the Cross yet? Are you ready to pick up your Cross daily and follow Him to whom you have submitted and serve others? Do you truly understand the difficulty of the sacrifices that you will be required to make? If you are still ready to take a stand, then let us begin the training necessary to walk the walk of a dedicated Christian soldier. Forward Yo-o!

4

4:1 I Entreat You

"Therefore I, the prisoner of the Lord, implore you to walk in a manner worthy of the calling, with which you have been called". (Eph. 4:1)

Because God is to be given glory in the Church, Paul is asking us to listen carefully to his words. The word "entreat" is pronounced *"par-ak-al-EH-o"* in the Greek language and means to call to someone in a polite manner, requesting him or her to move next to you.

It is not the command of a superior, but the request of a friend.

The Bible tells us in Ecclesiastes 3:1 that "there is an appointed time for everything." This indicates that the same Scriptural instruction may take on different significances for the different seasons, or stages of maturity, of your Christian lives. There were times when Jesus preached from a boat; removed from the multitudes, and other times, like in Matthew 15:10, that "He called the multitude to Him." There are times when preaching and teaching should be done with absolute apostolic authority. At these times the Bible's commands are to be given as though they were being uttered by the very voice of God. However, in the present case, Paul is merely saying, "Come here, pal. Let me put my arm around you as we walk, and let us always be conscious of the example we set as witnesses for Christ in whatever mission God assigns us to do. God is able to provide exceedingly and abundantly more than you can ask from Him or think about asking from Him. He deserves glory from us, and I am asking you to glorify Him in all your undertakings."

The Calling

Paul's petition to you is to glorify God in every single thing that you do. Part of that glorifying takes the form of walking in a manner worthy of your calling. What is that calling with which we have been called? Upon closer inspection, it is not only the profession you have chosen—by which you earn your income—but also the calling to receive forgiveness from God who called you to be forgiven to be saved, and to become a Christian. In Romans 8:30, it says, "Whom He predestined, these He also called; and whom He called, these He also justified." Those who have been called have been justified. Justified means that your guilt has been erased. To say, "I am justified," means, "My guilt has been removed. It is as though I had never sinned. or, "just as if I'd" never sinned, my guilt has been removed." And since you have been called and are now sinless and have no sin recorded in God's eyes, you can be admitted into Heaven. That's why the writer of Hebrews told you in Hebrews 3:1, we are "partakers of a heavenly calling." Paul told Timothy to "take hold of the eternal life to which you were called" (1 Tim. 6:12). That makes it clear, doesn't it? God called you and then justified you. You've been called with a heavenly calling; you've been called to eternal life. Have you responded?

In a Manner Worthy

So, to glorify God, Paul is directing you as a friend to walk worthy of this calling. This delineates a major turning point in Ephesians, a dividing line between the first half and the second half of the letter, between doctrine and exhortation, between teaching and preaching or, as I like to think of it, between boot camp and combat training. While, I do like the simple and accurate way that Jim West explains it; I'd like to paraphrase him if I can. In short, West indicates that God is teaching you in chapters 1–3 that He has made each of you a saint and taught you how to talk the talk. In chapters 4–6, He will teach you how to live a saintly life and walk the Christian walk.

Paul points out that you are to be walking in a worthy manner, but what does worthy mean? Worthy means "to be comparable" or "to weigh the same." Paul is telling you the weight you place on your walk should be the same as the weight you place on your calling. In other words, the effort expended living your Christian life should equal the effort spent adhering to or defining the standards of Christianity. Your behavior before God should always attempt to match the grace you've received from God, even though there is no possibility it ever will. The mission statement is simply, if you decide to talk the talk, then you better be able to walk the walk.

Walk

So what does an unprejudiced walk—the type of walk you are supposed to walk—look like? How does it appear when your walk weighs the same as your calling? Here are some clues toward recognizing it, straight from the Scripture, in the form of do's and don'ts:

Don'ts:

> "Do not walk according to the flesh, but according to the Spirit." (Rom. 8:4)
>
> "Not walking in craftiness or adulterating the Word of God." (2 Cor. 4:2)

Do's:

"Walk in a manner worthy of the Lord...please [Him] in all respects, bearing fruit in every good work and increasing in the knowledge of God."(Col. 1:10)

"Walk in good works." (Eph. 2:10)

"Walk as wise men." (Eph. 5:15)

"Walk in newness of life." (Rom. 6:4)

"Walking according to love." (Rom. 14:15)

"Walk by faith, not by sight." (2 Cor. 5:7)

"Walk according to His commandments." (2 John 6)

"Walk as children of light." (Eph. 5:8)

"Walk in Him." (Col. 2:6)

"Walk and please God." (1 Thess. 4:1)

"Walk in the light." (1 John 1:7)

"Walking in truth." (2 John 4)

What it comes down to is the order issued by John to "walk in the same manner as He walked" (1 John 2:6). Walking like Jesus will put you into conflict with your own will, precipitating a commonly asked and quite popular question: What would Jesus do (WWJD)? While it is not wrong to ask, and certainly WWJD is a valid question, but before answering it you must consider your mission, "walking worthy of Christ's calling", and just what it means to walk as Christ walked. No matter how much you want to give into temptation, no matter how often that question is asked, you must never forget the answer, and the answer will always be the same: Jesus would always do the right thing, no matter how difficult or unpopular that decision might be.. Therefore, your "pat acronymic response" will always be, "Do the right thing," or "DTRT."

Now let's approach the Lord in prayer and ask Him to reveal to you where there is a discrepancy between your calling and your walk, and then you can commit to applying the same weight to them both.

Selah (Ground your gear and take time to pause and reflect.)

We may seem to have been advancing at a slow pace up to this point in our study of the book of Ephesians, but that is only because there is so much good material to contemplate. If truth be told, I have already accepted the fact that God's Word is so dynamic that even when I put this manuscript to bed for the final time, I will not have even scratched the surface of all the things God was trying to bless us with through His servant Paul. As chapter three ended and chapter four begins, Paul is in essence saying, "Because God is to be given glory in the Church, that means among all of us corporately, and in each of us individually, I ask you, as a friend, to make sure that your Christian walk is of the same weight as your Christian calling." I know it is hard, but if you turn that walk and talk over to the Holy Spirit, then you'll be "walkin' in tall cotton," as they say down South. But even walkin' in tall cotton is not pain free since cotton plants can still scratch you.

I am not going to complete Paul's last thought yet, but I will attempt to finish his sentence as I see it applied in my life. Let's read Ephesians 4:1 again to see the first part of that sentence, "I, therefore, the prisoner of the Lord, entreat you to walk in a manner worthy of the calling with which you have been called."Now, "lets get crackin' times a waistin'."

4:2–3 While You

> "...with all humility and gentleness, with patience, showing tolerance for one another in love, being diligent to preserve the unity of the Spirit in the bond of peace." (Eph. 4:2–3)

Paul's focus here is on the unity of the Body of Christ, and in the next verses you will examine he says, "While you are walking worthy of your calling, please be mindful of your relationships with other folks in and out of the Church family."

I know beyond any shadow of a doubt that this message is very applicable to the Church today. Because it almost always seems the larger a congregation grows, the better the odds become that a person will find themselves face to face (or pew to pew) with people that they feel they can't get along with. For example, maybe next Sunday you'll find yourself sitting next to the guy from work, yeah him, the one guy at work that you really don't get along with, or the kid who crunched your daughter's car in the high school parking lot a few months ago and tried to get out of repairing the damage. Now you are asking yourself the question, "What are they doing at *my* church?" (Who's church?) Maybe you spot someone you've gone head-to-head with in the past, or maybe someone was there last week, someone that you have no history with, but you just plain don't like from the first time you set eyes on him or her. The larger a church congregation grows the more you're going to be challenged to grow as a Christian. So Paul provides you with a list of things you need to be aware of and continuously working on, beginning with humility and transitioning through gentleness, patience, and love.

Humility

Humility is a funny thing. It means to have a modest opinion of oneself. It is the opposite of pride. The Bible warns you that someone should not "think more highly of himself than he ought to think" (Rom. 12:3). But in our minds, yours and mine, we often think—declaring to the world in both word and attitude—in this way: "Fortunately, the fact that I am as great as I really am means I couldn't possibly think more highly of myself than I ought to!" or "I'm actually very proud of how humble I am." Even Nashville failed to understand the Apostle Paul when a country music lyricist wrote, "Oh Lord, it's hard to be humble when you're perfect in every way." Do you have a handle on how God detests pride? Satan sure does. You better understand that because who among you could even appear proud standing before God? Not a single soul I know, including me.

But let's get back to the point: we're talking right now about humility in the Church body. and to be perfectly honest, it is really easy to be proud when you're around other human beings because most human beings cannot come close to measuring up to your own opinion of yourself. In your mind, you're better looking, more educated, funnier, more informed, blessed with more common sense, and of more value to the world than most other people. You can't figure out how you got so lucky. You think God broke the mold when He made you. Take a good look around: He broke the mold when he formed each one of us. You may think, "I've got a great voice," but do you consider what others think? You think, "I play the guitar so well," but when others hear one of your recordings, what do they think? You think, "I look so good," so naturally, when you see your photograph you say, "Have you ever wondered how the camera adds ten pounds to a person?" It's really only putting back the ten pounds that your mind shaves off each time you look at yourself in the mirror! Folks, when you get right down to it, in reality, you're all pretty much the same when it comes to humility, and if you would take your minds off of how great you think you are for a while and start appreciating the many outstanding qualities of others, then you would be a great deal closer to walking with true humility. Remember what Paul told the Philippians in Philippians 2:3, "With humility of mind let each of you regard one another as more important than himself."

Gentleness

Paul's next concern is gentleness, as being gentle to one another does not apparently come naturally to many people. People can be so brutal at times, mowing others down like a fuel-injected Weed Eater plows through tall grass. Remember, if you will, God, not man, has set the standard of gentleness for us in Isaiah 40:11, "Like a shepherd He will tend His flock, in His arm He will gather the lambs, and carry them in His bosom; He will gently lead the nursing ewes." Our God treats us gently, even when we may not deserve it. "He speaks to us in the sound of a gentle blowing, a still small voice" (1 Kings 19:12, KJV and NASB). The Lord Jesus Christ has set the example of how we should conduct ourselves. He said in Matthew 11:29, "Learn from Me, for I am gentle and humble in heart."

"But Lord, really, come on now, You don't expect a Christian to show gentleness to people who are living their lives in sin, right? I can really "whup up" on them, right?" Wrong. Even when dealing with folks who have sinned grievously, the Bible cautions you in Galatians 6:1, "You who are spiritual, restore such a one in a spirit of gentleness." You might be saying, "But what about people who are complete hardheads, you know, those morons who won't get it if I'm gentle with them? After all, You are a Great and Mighty Warrior; you are even called a God of War; You know I can't get my point across to them by being a wimp!" Guess again, my friend. It is written of Jesus your High Priest in Hebrews 5:2 that "He can deal gently with the ignorant and misguided."

Whoever it is, whatever the situation, you need to let gentleness be your cloak. Even in conflict, as Proverbs 15:1 tells you, "A gentle answer turns away wrath, but a harsh word stirs up anger." To be perfectly honest, gentleness is far from second nature for me. I have no doubt God wired me to be a warrior. Having been in the military and law enforcement my entire adult life (more than 40 years is all I'll say) and I am still carrying a badge. I'm much better at understanding the wrath and anger things than the gentle answer stuff. Still, I can't ignore those things just because they are difficult for me to grasp. So Paul coaches and chides me, along with the Holy Spirit when necessary, reminding me that gentleness is something I need to pursue. 1 Timothy 6:11 says, "But thou, O man of God, flee these things; and follow after righteousness, godliness, faith, love, patience, meekness all of which contributes to developing gentleness." I have learned to count on that gentleness to carry me through many conflicts not all of my own choosing, during some very critical times in my law enforcement career. It seems like the calm and peace that covers me, along with the excellent training I have received, have allowed God to use me as He wants to use you: to bring the message of peace, compassion, and salvation to others in their times of greatest need. I could tell you story after story of the ways in which God has used me, but that would be another book., so let me get back on track.

Patience

Next up on your list is patience. Ouch! Ouch! And double ouch!

James said that people are always going to try your patience, and boy was he right! In James 5:9–11 he says:

> "Do not complain, brethren, against one another, that you yourselves may not be judged; behold, the Judge is standing right at the door. As an example, brethren, of suffering and patience, take the prophets who spoke in the name of the Lord. Behold, we count those blessed who endured. You have heard of the endurance of Job and have seen the outcome of the Lord's dealings that the Lord is full of compassion and [is] merciful."

I am a perfect example of someone who often finds they lack the required patience when dealing with people. This is not an acceptable trait in either of my chosen professions, and it has taken the power of God through the wisdom and omnipresence of the Holy Spirit to keep me performing as a witness for Christ in the most trying and chaotic circumstances. Sometimes this lack of patience happens even to people in the church.

Let's look at Job's friends. With friends like them, the saying goes, who needs enemies? Could you have shown patience to them? We can also look at the prophets. They preached unremittingly to God's people, yet God's people perpetually tried their patience too. Job, however, endured in spite of his friends and so did the prophets, in spite of the lack of respect they received. How did they do it? They did it by frequently displaying divine amounts of patience. I know you must have heard the old adage, "Don't pray for patience!" People who say this think that God will send all kinds of trials and difficulties your way in order for you to learn patience, and they don't look forward to those trials. In reality, living in this world is enough to test anyone's patience! Just about every circumstance and situation and every interaction with other human beings (yes, I am even talking about some of those in church) can try your patience to its limit. My philosophy is to pray for patience. I hope that God will grant it to me and that I'll have it available for the inevitable trials that will come my way. I want to be properly trained and equipped for every battle before it begins. Besides, James advises you to take joy in trials because they will only strengthen you. You ought to remember that the sharpest and longest-lasting edge can only be placed on tempered steel, steel that is immersed in fire.

Forbearance in Love

We are also admonished to show forbearance in love. Forbearance means tolerance. In other words, sometimes people in or out of the church have to be endured. You are saying, "But Lord, how can I put up with such an exasperating person? A person with such an uncompromising personality? Such a rabble-rouser?" The Lord's response is simple and eternal: love. Jesus said in John 15:12, "This is My commandment, that you love one another, just as I have loved you." Jesus loves you even though you may bear a striking resemblance to the person you just described. He has put up with so much from you, and He has never left nor forsaken you, even when you were as insufferable as the Pharisees. Now He's telling you to do likewise with one another. Endure with love. 1 Corinthians 13:4–7 says:

> "Love is patient, love is kind, [and] is not jealous; love does not brag [and] is not arrogant, does not act unbecomingly; it does not seek its own, is not provoked, does not take into account a wrong [suffered,]

does not rejoice in unrighteousness, but rejoices with the truth; bears
all things, believes all things, hopes all things, endures all things."

When you refuse to show the required tolerance, you're refusing to love,
and rejecting Christ's command. There will be times in your Christian life
that God will not want you to be tolerant of things because they run in direct
opposition to His plans. He will reveal to you at the appropriate time certain
things that must not be tolerated. Tolerance of these things would eventually
lead to their acceptance as a false standard of measurement for the Church and
the secular world, but we'll address them another time.

Being Conscientious

You are also being told that if you are diligent in these things we have been
discussing, unity will be preserved, and peace will endure and bind us together.
So don't just read these things, apply yourselves to these things. Be humble
and exalt other people in the Church and be patient with them because they
are probably being patient with you. Show self-control and endure difficult
people with love because for all you know, you might be the person that someone else is enduring. When unity is achieved through peace, you can only then
truly understand the Bible's words in Romans 12:5, "We, who are many, are
one body in Christ and individually members one of another."

Selah (Ground your gear, take time to pause and reflect.)

Paul is in the middle of his idea that the Church needs to glorify God, and,
in order for that to happen, the Church needs to be getting along harmoni-
ously with one another. We've talked before about the ideas of having humility, being gentle, practicing patience, and showing leniency to one another in
love. If you're being conscientious about these things, then you will be preserving the unity of the body. Along the same lines, Paul is about to point out to
us just how and why we are united. So what are we doing goldbrickin', coffee
break's over, let's get back in the battle.

4:4–7 One Body

"There is one body and one Spirit, just as also you were called in one
hope of your calling; one Lord, one faith, one baptism, one God and
Father of all who is over all and through all and in all. But to each

one of us grace was given according to the measure of Christ's gift".
(Eph. 4:4–7)

Unity within the Church shouldn't be that difficult to obtain. After all, if you're really being attentive to preserving that bond of peace, then the rest should be easy. If you've already got a common bond with one another, then maintaining it should be easy, right? I wish things were that simple. In spite of the fact that there are many church buildings and many church denominations, there really is just one Church, and that's the first thing Paul is talking about on his list of things we Christians have in common. Ephesians 4:4 says, "There is one body." Throughout the Scriptures, the Church is called "the Body of Christ." For example, Colossians 1:18 says, "He is also head of the body, the church." Colossians 1:24 says, "His body (which is the church)."

Because Jesus Christ is no longer physically on earth, Christians are His hands and arms, and His feet and legs. They are His body. He is the head, directing the movement, but they are doing the physical part. There's one body, one Church, and everyone in the world is either a part of the Body of Christ, or they're not. So regardless of the unbelievably divergent things that Christians believe, practice, and think, the fact remains true that there is but one Body of Christ. Some denominations believe some things, others don't. But the Church is the Church is the Church. There is one body. There are not two bodies, Catholic and Protestant. There is one body. There are not three bodies: pre-tribulation rapture, mid-tribulation rapture, and post-tribulation rapture. There is one body. There are not four bodies: Southern, General, American, and Independent. There is one body. So remember, one Church, one Body of Christ, and you're either in it or you're not. I tend to put it this way: you may display a North Carolina, Florida, California, or Texas license plate on your car and probably even have some sense of pride in your home state, but over and above all, you are an American sharing a strong sense of American values with every other American, no matter what license plate they display on their vehicle. When you are overseas, you are more likely to respond to an inquiry about your origin by stating you are an American rather than a Californian, a Virginian, or even a Texan. It should be the same way in the Church. There is only one Cross that we all focus on, one Calvary, and there is only one Jesus. If you believe that Jesus, the Son of God, is the Way, the Truth, and the Life, that he died on that cross for your sins and left you His inerrant word in the Bible, and that only by Him shall you enter Heaven, then what heavenly good will it do to bicker and separate over the dogma of man?

One Spirit

There is only one way a person can get into that one Church: they must be born-again. Yes, you must be born of the Holy Spirit. When anyone recognizes that they are a sinner and are separated from God, and they choose to believe that Jesus Christ (God's Own Son and the second person of the Holy Trinity) died on the Cross and suffered the death penalty for their sin in order to pay their sacrificial ransom, they are born-again by God's Holy Spirit. You are part of the Church only because God, as He said through His Word in 2 Corinthians 1:22, "Sealed us and gave [us] the Spirit in our hearts as a pledge." No, there shouldn't be any trouble with unity in the body because everyone who is in the body is of the same Spirit. That's why Paul said this in Ephesians 4:4, "One Spirit." Never forget that there is more than one Spirit in creation. There are evil spirits out there as well, and Paul tells you that these are the enemies whom we fight. Not only Paul, but the Spirit warned us about these other spirits in 1 Timothy 4:1, "But the Spirit explicitly says that in later times some will fall away from the faith, paying attention to deceitful spirits and doctrines of demons." There are many spirits out there who want to lead you down the wrong path. Still, as far as the Body of Christ is concerned, there is only one Spirit, which you follow.

Our One Hope

Next, Paul says in Ephesians 4:4, "Just as also you were called in one hope of your calling."

Aside from one body and one Spirit, there is one hope. What is that hope Paul is referring to? It is possible that searching without the wisdom or leading of the Holy Spirit may result in some confusion. After all, the Bible does talk about many hopes. Acts 23:6 mentions "the hope and resurrection of the dead!" Galatians 5:5 talks about "the hope of righteousness." Colossians 1:5 discusses "the hope laid up for you in heaven." Colossians 1:27 talks about "the hope of glory." Titus 1:2 promises "the hope of eternal life." At first it sounds like there are many hopes, doesn't it? Yet if you look at them closely, you will see that they are all in fact related, and there is only one hope: hope that we place in the finished work of Jesus Christ. This hope will raise us from the dead to eternal life in Heaven, in glory and righteousness forever and ever! This is referring to everyone who is one in the Body of Christ, to those who have been sealed by the one Spirit. They are the ones clinging to this one eternal hope.

One Lord

Paul then mentions, "One Lord" (Eph. 4:5). Remember, we learned back in chapter one that the word "Lord" is a respectful title, meaning "master, possessor or owner," coming from a root word meaning "supremacy." By now we should recognize that Jesus Christ is our Lord. That is why He is called in Revelation 19:16 the, "KING OF KINGS, AND LORD OF LORDS." However, the very fact that He is the "Lord of Lords" tells us that there is more than one Lord. There are many Lords in people's lives that seem to control or master them. People may be owned by, or in submission to, dozens of different things. A driving desire for money, a physical or psychological addiction to drugs, obsessive dependence on personal relationships, a fanatical quest for fame and glory, a passionate desire for power, all these often display a mastery and lordship over many people's lives.

When you make the profession of faith that states Jesus is your Lord, He is to be the only Lord you serve. He warned against trying to live in this world in Matthew 6:24, "No one can serve two masters; for either he will hate the one and love the other, or he will hold to one and despise the other." You cannot serve both God and man. There can be no divided allegiance within a single body; you can only be owned and led by one master. You can only acknowledge and serve one Lord. If you desire unity in the Body of Christ, it will only come if your corporate hearts are not divided, and you are not busy serving other masters.

One Faith

Paul speaks in Ephesians 4:5 about "one faith." In the world we live in, this is not a very popular way of thinking. The world today is constantly trying to program us to accept all faiths. But the Bible never condones a general faith, or any old faith. The Bible only validates "The faith." The faith that is called "The faith" is more than a namby-pamby faith in a god of your choice or a god of your own making. It is only faith in our Lord Jesus Christ that is true faith (as is written in Acts 20:21, 24:24; Rom. 3:22, 3:26; Gal. 2:16, 3:22, 3:26; Eph. 1:15; Col. 1:4; Rev. 14:12, etc.). Above all else, there is no provision for man to become enlightened enough to elevate himself to a position equal to God in any form or fashion, as some would have us believe. Satan thought he could become like God, and that's exactly what got him into the mess he is in today. Do you want to make the same mistake he made? I don't. My faith is in the Lord and, as long as I exercise it, my faith will remain strong.

One Baptism

Then Paul tells us in Ephesians 4:5 that there is but "one baptism." There is as you have come to expect, some controversy surrounding these two words in Scripture due in part to the fact that the Bible mentions many kinds of baptisms: John's baptism of repentance, Jesus' baptism, the baptism of the Holy Spirit and fire, baptism into death, the cultic practice of baptism for the dead, and the Jewish practice of baptizing those whom they proselytized. I think Paul's other writings clarify which baptism he is speaking of, however, and a clue can be found in 1 Corinthians 12:13–14, "For by one Spirit we were all baptized into one body, whether Jews or Greeks, whether slaves or free, and we were all made to drink of one Spirit. For the body is not one member, but many." This reference to one baptism I believe, is the baptism into the Body of Christ. No one gets into the Body of Christ apart from the Holy Spirit entering their lives and hearts and sealing them with God's seal of ownership.

One God and Father

Now to really get the blood flowing, *God* is God. Allah is not God. Buddha is not God. Mohammed is not God. The Virgin Mary is not God. Confucius is not God. Joseph Smith is not God, and even a great man like Billy Graham is not God. We are not gods nor will we ever become gods, no matter what the New Age followers say. Keep in mind that New Age is a misleading term since the idea of becoming a god is far from new and definitely not limited to our age. There is only one God and Father. The Bible confirms this in many places. For instance, 1 Timothy 2:5–6 says, "For there is one God, [and] one mediator also between God and men, [the] man Christ Jesus, who gave Himself as a ransom for all." Jesus said in John 14:6, "I am the way, and the truth, and the life; no one comes to the Father but through Me."

Up to now, as we've seemingly crawled our way through Ephesians, it seems clear that one thing has become evident: there is only one Way. There's only one real Church, one Spirit, one hope, one Lord and Master, one true faith, one baptism, and one true God that you need to come to. He has provided only one way to Him: through belief in His one and only Son, Jesus Christ.

Grace

When you draw near to God in this way, He gives you His grace, the gift of Jesus Christ. In Romans 6:23, Paul draws a clear and simple picture for the Romans when he tells them, "For the wages of sin is death, but the free gift of God is eternal life in Christ Jesus our Lord."

Selah (Ground your gear, take time to pause and reflect.)

Reflect quietly on this for a moment. Paul has been writing about the unity we as Christians have in Christ. His most recent account of things that we have in common as believers deals with each of us having been given the gift of God's grace. When he finishes that thought, its importance seems to strike him, and he decides to devote another two or three sentences toward what he considers to be an "essential digression." I love that term. I think that is what happens to me every time I try and give a public talk. I essentially digress to what the Holy Spirit feels is more essential than I originally did when I wrote my presentation notes. Well, Paul's detour, not mine, is where we'll direct our next instructional emphasis. Paul's trigger for turning down this proverbial rabbit trail was Ephesians 4:7, "But to each one of us grace was given according to the measure of Christ's gift." As Paul meditated on his thoughts regarding the source of that grace and that Christ gave us that special gift, he began to think about the exceptional gift of eternal life that Christ bestowed on some other folks. OK, troops, if you want to find out who they were, grab your gear and let's get back in the war, 'cuz time's a waistin'.

4:8–10 First He Descended

"Therefore it says, 'WHEN HE ASCENDED ON HIGH, HE LED CAP-TIVE A HOST OF CAPTIVES, AND HE GAVE GIFTS TO MEN." (Now this expression, "He ascended," what does it mean except that He also had descended into the lower parts of the earth? He who descended is also He who ascended far above all the heavens, so that He might fill all things.) (Eph. 4:8–10)

Paul has quoted a verse from Psalm 68, which prophetically proclaimed the ascension of Jesus Christ and that He ascended to Heaven after he rose from the dead. Even so, before He ascended, Jesus first had to descend. Where, you may be asking, did Jesus descend? We do not have to wonder very long because, before being arrested and crucified, Jesus Himself prophesied, "Just as Jonah was three days and three nights in the belly of the sea monster, so shall the Son of Man be three days and three nights in the heart of the earth" (Matt. 12:40). And when Jesus was crucified on Calvary, a man named Joseph of Arimathea "took the body and wrapped it in a clean linen cloth, and laid it in his own new tomb, which he had hewn out in the rock; and he rolled a large stone against the entrance of the tomb" (Matt. 27:59–60).

Jesus' body was placed in the earth, but that's not the only thing that was happening. Things were being chronicled that no one on earth could witness. You see, He wasn't just placed in the earth, but in fulfillment of the prophecy, Jesus Himself descended into the heart of the earth. Now, let me try to make this a little clearer for you. Jesus did not go and suffer in hell's fire. I have heard some dissenting, and in my mind it is profane and sacrilegious. Some preachers declare how awful it is that Jesus descended to be tormented in hell for our sins. According to the Bible, that is clearly not the case. On the Cross, Jesus said, "It is finished!" (John 19:30). If He was going to suffer for three days in hell, then He might likely have quoted a line from a future hit song, "It's only just begun." And never would he have said to the "good" thief, "Verily I say unto thee, today shalt thou be with me in paradise" (Luke 23: 43). No, I don't think my Lord, who is so compassionate and merciful, is the kind who would have invited that redeemed sinner to join him in the fires of hell. Not a God who has promised all sinners who are born again into the Body of Christ, a freedom from facing the lake of fire. I think it is a sure thing that, when Jesus went to the heart of the earth, He went in victory not in defeat.

The Heart of the Earth

As was foretold in both the Old and New Testaments, Jesus descended into the heart of the earth only to ascend again. Although He went down alone, He brought back an army! We are told He led a host of captives. Have you ever wondered or even asked someone, "What were these folks doing in the heart of the earth, and why were they there?" To get a clearer understanding of the answer to that question, we will need to turn to Luke 16. That is where Jesus told the story of the rich man and Lazarus. Luke 16:19–23 says:

> "Now there was a certain rich man, and he habitually dressed in purple and fine linen, gaily living in splendor every day. And a certain poor man named Lazarus was laid at his gate, covered with sores,

and longing to be fed with the [crumbs] which were falling from the rich man's table; besides, even the dogs were coming and licking his sores. Now it came about that the poor man died and the angels to Abraham's bosom carried him away; and the rich man also died and was buried. And in Hades he lifted up his eyes, being in torment, and saw Abraham far away, and Lazarus in his bosom."

We need to take a close look at the significance of this story. Two men died, and both were taken down into the heart of the earth. One man was in torment, but the other was comforted. Scripture says Lazarus was in Abraham's bosom, a place that Jesus called Paradise. It also appears to say, while Lazarus was in a place without torment, just across the abyss the rich man was not. Luke 16:24 says, "And he cried out and said, 'Father Abraham, have mercy on me, and send Lazarus, so that he may dip the tip of his finger in water and cool off my tongue, for I am in agony in this flame.'" Paul also tells the Colossians what happened when Jesus descended into the heart of the earth in Colossians 2:15, "When He had disarmed the rulers and authorities, He made a public display of them, having triumphed over them through Him." The rulers and authorities of the underground were demonic powers in the spiritual realm. Jesus disarmed them and made a public display of them.

A Host of Captives

A public display always requires a public audience. In other words, Jesus' triumph had to take place in front of people. Remember, in Paradise, there were Lazarus, Abraham, and many others who had lived their lives by faith in God prior to the ministry of Jesus. Even though they had faith, they were still sinners like the rest of us. They, like all of us, were not sinless and perfect. You do realize, I hope, that faith is the only way a person can be granted admission into Heaven. These Faithful people were well-treated prisoners of war (POW) in Abraham's bosom. They were being comforted yet still held captive. They were faithful people but not yet forgiven people. Fortunately, when Jesus died, He paid the price of sin for all who place their hope in Him.

When that happened, captivity itself could be taken captive. Jesus was thus able to escort these internees of the spiritual war of good and evil from their captivity in the heart of the earth.

Gifts He Gave to Men

Jesus not only freed them but also gave them gifts. He gave them, as he also gives you, the gifts of grace, righteousness, and eternal life. Romans 3:24 tells of "being justified as a gift by His grace through the redemption which is in Christ Jesus;" Romans 5:17 mentions "those who receive the abundance of grace and of the gift of righteousness will reign in life through the One, Jesus Christ." Romans 5:15 talks about "the gift by the grace of the one Man, Jesus Christ." It is said in Ephesians 4:7, "To each one of us grace was given according to the measure of Christ's gift." Jesus granted this gift to all who were in Abraham's bosom, waiting for the Messiah to appear on earth and repatriate them.

Then He Ascended

Jesus could not have freed them and led them up to Heaven if He were not still alive, now could He? We all know that Jesus died on the Cross in order to ransom us from the death penalty we each deserve. So how does someone rise from the dead? The Bible teaches us that death entered the world through sin (Rom. 5:12). Sin reigns in death (Rom. 5:21), and the sting of death is sin (1 Cor. 15:56). Jesus never sinned; He was completely sinless. So death could exercise no claim on Him. That's why the Bible says "And God raised Him up again, putting an end to the agony of death, since it was impossible for Him to be held in its power" (Acts 2:24). Do you see it now? Jesus rose from the dead because in Him there was no sin to hold Him in death. You're going to die someday, but there is a way we can keep death from having any power over us. But there is only one way, my friend, and John tells you what Jesus said in John 11:25–26, "I am the resurrection and the life; he who believes in Me shall live even if he dies, and everyone who lives and believes in Me shall never die." When you truly believe in Jesus, all of your past, present, and future sins are forgiven, thus death no longer wields its power over you either. You are told in 1 Corinthians 15:54–57—and not in Shakespeare, "'DEATH IS SWALLOWED UP in victory. 'O DEATH, WHERE IS YOUR VICTORY? O DEATH, WHERE IS YOUR STING?'" For Christians, gone forever is the sting of death that is found in sin, and the power of sin that is the law. Thanks be to God, who gives us the victory over sin and death through our Lord Jesus Christ. You have won the victory because, just as Jesus rose up over death into Heaven, you too who have received forgiveness for your sins will ascend to Heaven when you die.

Selah (Ground your gear, take time to pause and reflect.)

Paul, with a few "essential digressions," has been writing about unifying the Church. When we go back out on patrol, we will be covering how God has established a system within His Church that is designed to guide you toward unity. So when you're ready to mount up and stop dilly-dallying, let me know, and we'll head up and move out.

It's about time you learn where God wants you to be assigned and what He wants you to do for him.

4:11–13 Time for Your Commission and Branch Designation

"And He gave some as apostles, and some as prophets, and some as evangelists, and some as pastors and teachers, for the equipping of the saints for the work of service, to the building up of the Body of Christ; until we all attain to the unity of the faith, and of the knowledge of the Son of God, to a mature man, to the measure of the stature which belongs to the fullness of Christ." (Eph. 4:11–13)

"He gave…" The "He" spoken of here is Jesus Christ. He gave these gifted individuals to the Church as ministers whose assignments were to build up the Body of Christ, which is the Church itself. That was His promise to Peter as recorded in Matthew 16:18, "I will build My church; and the gates of Hades shall not overpower it." Jesus is the One who builds His Church, and remember it is His Church. He is the One who gives the assignments to those who minister to the Church. That's why, when men take charge of the process and people appoint themselves to ministry, disaster frequently follows. Solomon wrote in Psalm 127:1, "Unless the LORD builds the house, they labor in vain who build it." The Church is to be built by Jesus. When someone decides, "I have a better way of doing things than we have here," or as I have been witness to three times, in church splits, someone gets the idea they can do things better than their pastor (whom God gave them) and says, "I'm going to take as many of these people as I can convince to come with me and start my own church." It should not come as a surprise to anyone that none of these congregations got their leadership from God, and, consequently, their subsequent collapse was imminent. Any church that Jesus doesn't build isn't even a church, because it is certainly not the house of God.

Four Offices

There are several offices, gifts, ministries, or commissions (whichever you prefer to call them) that Jesus established for the building and edification of His Church. Paul tells us they are apostles, prophets, evangelists, pastors, and teachers. Most, if not all, of these terms can be misunderstood for several reasons, so let's take some time to learn a little about them.

Apostles

First on Paul's list is the apostle. I can't tell you how many books there are that say this office was exclusively a ministry distinctive of the early Church. Most Christians don't think twice when a preacher parrots this hypothesis, responding with, "Well, of course we know that, the apostles are long-gone. Because, as you know, there were only the twelve." Seldom does someone question such a statement. But the word "apostle" merely means "one who is sent out." And of course you know that Jesus sent out the original twelve guys who were called apostles. But don't forget, when Judas hung himself, Matthias was appointed to fill his place. That makes thirteen. Then Paul was called an apostle, and that makes fourteen. In fact, there were lots of other men who were called apostles: Barnabas (Acts 14:14), *An-DRON-ee-kos* and *Ee-oo-NEE-as* (Rom. 16:7), the Lord's brother, James (Gal. 1:19), and Silas and Timothy (1 Thess. 1:1 with 2:6). They all became apostles, having been sent out to plant churches and establish the work of God in the world. Nowhere does the Bible say, "By the way, when this book is finished, so are the apostles. When the first century comes to an end, so will the last of the apostles." Certainly God is still sending people to cities and towns in this great country, preaching the Gospel and establishing churches. In fact, the word "apostle" translates as "ambassador," or one who carries a message, and there are definitely many ambassadors of Christ carrying the Gospel around the world in the form of church-planting and Bible-teaching missionaries.

Prophets

Next on Paul's list are prophets. These are people who receive a Word from the Lord and proclaim it. This word can come by supernatural revelation, vision, dream, or from the Word of God itself. The content of the prophecy always "speaks to men for edification and exhortation and consolation" (1 Cor. 14:3). The prophet edifies you, strongly warns you against sin, or reassures you with comfort. Once more, there are many who say there are no real prophets today, that the last prophet was John the Baptist. They quote Jesus as saying in Matthew 11:13, "For all the prophets and the Law prophesied until John." "So I guess that's it, no more prophets," they claim. Here is the problem. Paul is saying Jesus gave us prophets to equip the Church. The Church wasn't built until after John died, and it is still being equipped today. Ipso facto, if he were the last of the prophets, we would have a real problem! You can see prophets have continued on after John if you look at Acts 11:27–28, "Some prophets came down from Jerusalem to Antioch. And one of them named Agabus stood up and [began] to indicate by the Spirit that there would certainly be a great famine all over the world." Acts 13:1 says, "At Antioch, in the church that was there, prophets and teachers: Barnabas, and Simeon who was called Niger, and Lucius of Cyrene, and Manaen who had been brought up with Herod the Tetrarch, and Saul." Acts 15:32 says, "Judas and Silas, also being prophets themselves, encouraged and strengthened the brethren with a lengthy message." Additionally, the church in Corinth was told in 1 Corinthians 14:29 to "let two or three prophets speak, and let the others pass judgment." And the Thessalonians were told in 1 Thessalonians 5:20–21, "Do not despise prophetic utterances. But examine everything [carefully]; hold fast to that which is good." Once again, there is no biblical evidence that Jesus was going to terminate the office of prophet at any time during the church age. As a matter of fact, Zechariah 13 tells you that prophecy stops in the Millennium. It is also interesting to notice the crossover in these ministry descriptions. For example, Silas and Barnabas were both listed as apostles as well as prophets. These offices are, therefore, not mutually exclusive.

Evangelists

Paul then identifies evangelists. You may remember from our review in chapter one that the word "Gospel" in Greek is pronounced *yoo-ang-GHEL-ee-on*, which means "good news." Well, the Greek word for "evangelist" is pronounced *yoo-ang-ghel-is-TACE*, which translates as "the bringer of the good news." So we can say evangelists are the ones who bring us the Gospel of Jesus Christ. One such example would be Philip, who in Acts 21:8 was also known as "Philip the Evangelist." "He…went down to the city of Samaria and [began] proclaiming Christ to them" (Acts 8:5). Today there are many people who claim to be evangelists, but only those who are truly preaching the Good News of Christ are evangelists.

Pastor/Teachers

Finally, Paul states there are the pastors and teachers. This does not indicate two separate groups in the Greek language, but one. This is the way Kenneth Wuest, in his *Word Studies in the Greek New Testament* defines it:

> We have Granville Sharp's rule evidenced here, which says that when there are two nouns in the same case connected by a kai (and), the first noun having the article, the second noun not having the article, the second noun refers to the same thing the first noun does and is a further description of it.

The word "pastor" means "shepherd." Since believers are often portrayed biblically as sheep, it stands to reason the pastor should be compared to a shepherd, since he protects Christians from their spiritual enemies, cares for them, and feeds them the Word of God. Paul tells pastors in Acts 20:28, "Be on guard for yourselves and for all the flock, among which the Holy Spirit has made you overseers, to shepherd the church of God which He purchased with His own blood." Peter echoed this message when he commanded pastors in 1 Peter 5:2–3, "Shepherd the flock of God among you, exercising oversight not under compulsion, but voluntarily, according to [the will of] God; and not for sordid gain, but with eagerness; nor yet as lording it over those allotted to your charge, but proving to be examples to the flock." While the pastor/teacher is protecting the flock, he needs to watch out for himself and be sure of his motives for being a pastor. This office is not to be taken frivolously, as can be seen by the warning James gives in James 3:1, "Let not many [of you] become teachers, my brethren, knowing that as such we shall incur a stricter judgment." There are other references in the Bible that seem to deal with pastors and teachers as individual callings. I will not disagree with Christians who see them as separate callings. I do feel, however, that while all teachers need not become pastors, all pastors should have the gift of teaching.

Equipping the Saints

The motive Jesus has for giving us apostles, prophets, evangelists, and pastor/teachers is to prepare saints for your Christian duties and responsibilities. The evangelist presents the Gospel to you, and hopefully you get saved. But are you immediately equipped to serve? Yes, but not entirely well-trained, I'm afraid. While your childlike enthusiasm often encourages older believers, and the sharing of your newborn faith may indeed help the body grow, you are no more ready to wade into the fiercest of spiritual battles than any "Newbie" who has recently graduated from boot camp. It will still take time and the assistance of other more mature Christians who God has called and equipped to help you grow into a mature believer ready to pick up, put on, and efficiently use the "Full Armor of God." Now let's see how these saints help us be better equipped, shall we?

We know an apostle plants a church or, as we know it, a congregation. So how does that help equip you? Well, you then have a place where the Body of Christ gathers, fellowships, and communes in corporate forms of worship. It's a place to worship, praise, and serve God, and to find fellow Christians with whom to do all these things with! I think that helps, don't you?

The prophet proclaims God's revelation to you, building you up, exhorting you, or consoling you with wisdom or even a personal word from God. You are equipped when the prophet's word adds blessing or brings rebuke or reassurance. Their efforts may cause or help you to straighten up, release some unnecessary baggage, or refresh you, as needed. Once you are freed from encumbrance, you can begin to serve God more abundantly.

The evangelist carries the Gospel to the masses, reaching and influencing multitudes. He carries the truth in Christ's message of salvation. But while he may reach many who make a decision for Christ, the evangelist is seldom the person directly charged with carrying on the discipleship, edification, and training responsibilities of the new Christian. This nurturing commission is laid on the shoulders of the next office: the pastors and teachers.

The pastor/teacher instructs you in the Word of God. How does that equip you? When you are well-versed in the Word, you are better equipped to grow and mature as a Christian. The greater your knowledge of the Word and the greater your heart for God becomes, the more you can serve God by helping His people grow and mature the way you are. You are on your way to becoming one of God's training officers yourself.

There are too many congregations that think the pastor is the only one who is supposed to be doing the serving. In reality, he is supposed to be equipping you for service so that you can each serve one another. That's why the apostles said in Acts 6:2 that, "It is not desirable for us to neglect the Word of God in order to serve tables." And in Acts 6:4, "But we will devote ourselves to prayer, and to the ministry of the Word." I have served in many of the church bodies. I have been a part of shepherding and teaching, and now I am again serving by responding to the urging of the Holy Spirit and writing this commentary. If you are maturing at all as a result of what I am doing, then you are becoming better prepared to serve. It's as simple as that. It is a sad fact that less than half of the people who attend a church on a regular basis ever serve in some sort of ministry. The truth is almost every ministry in any church congregation could use anywhere from one to twenty additional workers, or as we are learning to call them in our study, Christian Soldiers. Our desire is to attain a unity of the faith, a maturity of the body, and experience the fullness of life in Christ, so let me encourage you to step up to the plate and get involved by offering your work of service to the church you attend.

Selah (Ground your gear, take time to pause and reflect.)

We have been listening to Paul tell us that Jesus provided the Church with apostles, prophets, evangelists, and pastor/teachers whose duty is to equip the saints for their works of service in building up the Body of Christ. Now listen up and pay attention as he tells us in verse 14 why this is important.

4:14 About the Result

"As a result, we are no longer to be children, tossed here and there
by waves and carried about by every wind of doctrine, by the trickery
of men, by craftiness in deceitful scheming." (Eph. 4:14)

In other words, Paul is telling you, "You are not going to be left as babes in Christ because Jesus gave you evangelists, teachers, and pastors to ensure you would be well-equipped." God has given you these people to preach the Gospel to you, to establish church bodies with which you may be affiliated, to edify you, to exhort you, to console you, and to teach the Word to you. He desires that you be properly equipped so that false teaching and false teachers or prophets will not deceive you.

Three Word Pictures

Paul uses a word picture to illustrate how false teaching deceives people. He points out that you are no longer to be children tossed here and there by waves, carried about by every wind of doctrine. I can identify with what Paul is trying to communicate through the picture he is painting with his words. Here's an example from my life to illustrate this point.

When I was about nineteen, I went with some of my Marine Corps friends to a well-known beach in Hawaii. There were no crowds, no lifeguards, just the three of us "Jarhead surfers" and our longboards (9' 6" Bing for any old surfers out there). We were ready for a day of nonstop fun. But not long after I got out into the water, I felt something was wrong. I knew I was out of my element. Even though I had surfed many "breaks" along the West Coast from Tarantula Flats and K-39 in Baja to "Steamer Lane" near San Francisco, I had never experienced surf like I was facing that day. The size of the waves, the incline of the beach, and a powerful "rip," combined to make some pretty ominous conditions. When the waves would build, they quickly ripped the water away from the beach, while building eight to ten-foot-high "cliffs of surf." The first wave I caught wasn't that big, so I thought, and I felt my confidence start to build. I was riding it near the curl and slicing along its sheer face. I felt like I was almost flying.

Then all of a sudden, I was flying—flying, that is, toward the bottom beneath me, with very little water below me to cushion my impact. The wave bounced me violently along the bottom, the skeg on my surfboard was destroyed, and I was tumbled over and over, receiving a few cuts and bruises all over as I was tumbled around. Then the wave crashed down over me, spinning me around until I didn't know which way was up. I tried to swim toward the surface, only to find, as I encountered the bottom, that in my disoriented condition I was heading in the wrong direction. Although I survived the incident intact, that turned out to be my only ride of the day. Paul's illustration says that when you're led astray by bad or incorrect Bible teaching and religious philosophies, you're just like I was that day. You are like a disoriented little child whose spiritual conviction is being bounced around by waves of the world and by the winds of change. You are led down the garden path by false teachings that often appear benign. You need to be cautious, and, as the Bible warns you, learn with a discerning spirit, or you may begin to build your future on tenuous doctrine, which ultimately proves fatal.

Violent Winds of Doctrine

Hopefully you can see the value of sound doctrine. You live in an especially tumultuous and turbulent time. Paul warned you long ago about the days you're in now when he told you in 2 Timothy 4:3–4, "For the time will come when they will not endure sound doctrine; but [wanting] to have their ears tickled, they will accumulate for themselves teachers in accordance to their own desires; and will turn away their ears from the truth, and will turn aside to myths." It never ceases to amaze me that even though you have been given that warning, many Christians are so regularly, easily, and willingly deceived by the turbulent winds of doctrine that blow so rampantly across our country. To me, these winds of change often smell like they blew across a latrine or landfill. Still, it seems like time after time, people line up to hear or buy the latest thing that's blow'n' in the wind. They seem to be blown away by the latest book or blown over by the latest anointing when, in reality, they're just being tossed about by the latest ill winds of questionable doctrine.

Paul's writings warn you about these doctrines. He calls them "strange doctrines" in 1 Timothy 1:3, "doctrines of demons" in 1 Timothy 4:1, and "different doctrines" in 1 Timothy 6:3. How can you tell if a doctrine is strange, different, or demonic? Well, first of all, if ministers are equipping the saints, they are responsible for how they equip others. If you haven't been equipped like you should be, then it will take a little more work on your part. The key to recognizing a false or corrupt doctrine is to test it against the Bible and see if it is biblical, and you can't know what's biblical unless you know what's in the Bible. If you know the Bible, when someone says, "God wants you to be healthy and wealthy," your response should be, "1 Timothy 6:7–9 tells me that, we have brought nothing into the world, so we cannot take anything out of it either. And if we have food and covering, with these we shall be content. But those who want to get rich fall into the snare of temptation and many foolish and harmful desires, which plunge men into ruin and destruction." If someone else says, "You need to follow the Old Testament laws," your response will be, "Acts 15:28–29 tells us that no greater burden than a few essentials has been laid upon us." When someone else claims the Holy Spirit is causing people to pass out or laugh uncontrollably, your response can be, "Galatians 5 tells us the fruit of the Spirit is self-control." If another person says Christians can be demon-possessed, you should be able to respond that 1 John 4:4 says greater is He who is in you than he who is in the world. If a person says to you that you have a "generational curse," you can respond with Ezekiel 18:20, "The son will not bear the punishment for the father's iniquity, nor will the father bear the punishment for the son's iniquity; the righteousness of the righteous will be upon himself, and the wickedness of the wicked will be upon himself." You will see, when you are properly equipped and use the right references that you will not be so tossed around by this deceit. You will not feel like a child tossed by waves and carried by chilly winds of false, ear-tickling doctrine.

Deceit of Men

Some of you might respond, "Now, Ray, aren't you using kind of strong language when you say that these doctrines are lies? Don't you think that the people who came up with this philosophy or theology may be just honestly mistaken?" No, I don't believe that. I believe anyone who has the Holy Spirit living within them, who is reading the Bible with a right spirit, and who has no ulterior motives or agendas will not fall into such unconcealed falsehoods, nor will he or she attempt to propagate them. The fact is, these doctrines are born out of dishonesty, craftiness, and devious scheming (all tried-and-true tactics of our accuser). "What will sell my books? What will give me position and authority to control people? What will make me wealthy and famous? What will provide me with the acclaim I desire or to be known as wiser than all other Bible teachers?" John warned against such heresies and winds of doctrines in 1 John 2:26, "These things I have written to you concerning those who are trying to deceive you." Paul said that these worldly-minded men are simply "peddlers of the Word of God" (2 Cor. 2:17), and "walking…in craftiness and adulterating the Word of God" (2 Cor. 4:2). In Proverbs 30:6 we are warned, "Do not add to His words Lest He reprove you, and you be proved a liar." Now use caution here, remember there is still danger in standing on the truth. You can become self-righteous, condescending, and even insensitive in your delivery of the truth. That's why Paul tells you emphatically here—

4:15–16 To Be Speaking the Truth in Love

…"but speaking the truth in love, we are to grow up in all aspects into Him who is the head, even Christ, from whom the whole body, being fitted and held together by what every joint supplies, according to the proper working of each individual part, causes the growth of the body for the building up of itself in love." (Eph. 4:15–16)

Opinions are not changed, nor are souls won by arguments. People who are deceived by false doctrines will not be won over through heated discussion. Instead, you must make sure that you are speaking the truth in love. And never forget that 1 Corinthians 13:4 says, "Love is patient, love is kind…and is not arrogant," or as 1 Corinthians 13:5 says, "Love does not act unbecomingly; it does not seek its own, is not provoked." Too many people who are able to get a handle on the truth fail dismally in trying to get a handle on love.

The Whole Body Working as One

When you are properly equipped and not deceived by winds of doctrine, then you're growing together as a body. Only then are all the parts in place, properly connected, and functioning correctly. That is God's desire for your fellowship, for each part individually to be in working order, connected together in love.

Selah (Ground your gear, take time to pause and reflect.)

Paul began chapter four by saying that we need to walk in a manner worthy of our calling. If you remember, that means to "weigh the same as," so we need to make sure our Christian walk carries the same weight as our Christian profession of faith. Without that, Paul said, we will not have unity in the Church. In Ephesians 4:17, Paul begins with the statement, "This I say therefore." In other words, "Because you will not have unity until you walk in a manner worthy of the calling, I'm giving you the following exhortation." Now gather your "Kit" and get ready for a little close-order drill because if you are going to be an integral part of God's Army when this training is over, you need to really be in step and paying attention. It is time to learn to march in cadence.

4:17–19 Affirm Together With the Lord

"So this I say, and affirm together with the Lord, that you walk no longer just as the Gentiles also walk, in the futility of their mind, being darkened in their understanding, excluded from the life of God because of the ignorance that is in them, because of the hardness of their heart; and they, having become callous, have given themselves over to sensuality for the practice of every kind of impurity with greediness." (Eph. 4:17–19)

I believe in my heart that it's not just Paul, but the Lord Himself who is saying, "Hey, Church, walk worthy." One thing you always need to keep in mind when reading the Bible is that you don't get to ignore the writings of people you don't like. There may be people who say, "I don't read the book of Revelation, because John was old and probably just having psychotic delusions, or I don't read James because I think he was too much of a legalist, or I don't like Paul because of his male chauvinistic, intolerant, and homophobic ideas." The fact is, when you reject any of those writings, you're rejecting God. 2 Peter 1:20–21 says, "But know this first of all, that no prophecy of Scripture is [a matter] of one's own interpretation, for no prophecy was ever made by an act of human will, but men moved by the Holy Spirit spoke from God." God has inspired and provided the entire Bible, line upon line, precept upon precept (Isa. 28:10–13). The whole counsel of God (Acts 20:27) is to be believed and received. The way I see it, Paul is reminding you here, "Hey, it's not just me. It's the Lord speaking, and I'm just agreeing."

Don't Walk as the Gentiles Walk

Well, what is it that God is saying? He is telling you that you aren't to walk as the Gentiles walk. In Paul's day, the majority of mankind had completely rejected God's way. They had pursued various passions, all of which we can see prominently pursued by Americans today. Things like greed, immorality, and power over others and a lack of ethical behavior; as I stop and think about it, society today appears to really be in step with that ancient gentile cadence.

Futility of Mind

Paul says the Ephesians walked in the futility of their mind. The word "futility," as used here, seems to translate as, "anything that is inappropriate, anything that is perverse, depraved, or devoid of truth." The Bible says that man's false religion (Acts 14:15; Titus 3:9; 1 Pet. 1:18) and man's wisdom (1 Cor. 3:20) are futile because they are perverted, rejecting God's Word, His will, and His way.

Darkened in Their Understanding

When someone gives their mind over to pointlessness, their understanding becomes darkened. The cartoon symbol for understanding, as you know, is a light bulb appearing over someone's head. "Badda-bing, badda-boom! The light just went on! Now I get it!" When you let your mind focus on the inappropriate and perverse things of this world, the electricity never starts flowing. Things just get darker and darker, and you never understand the life that God wants to provide for you. You just stumble along out of sync with the world and God, and you never realize what you're missing.

Ignorance

I don't care what the world says, ignorance is not bliss. Ignorance is ignorance, and no matter how you dress it up, a pig is still a pig. Where does spiritual ignorance come from? It's not that Muslims or Buddhists are dumb, or that evolutionary advocates lack intelligence, it is that their pursuit of futility obfuscates their understanding, which allows them to become pawns of ignorance. I find it interesting that the word "ignorance" comes from the Greek word pronounced *AG-noy-ah*, from which we get our word "agnostic." It means "to have a deficiency of knowledge." There are people I know who proudly state, "I am an agnostic, I have no knowledge or proof of God's existence." They must be deaf and blind!

Excluded from the Life God Planned

When a person's understanding is darkened, they have little or no knowledge of God, and they end up being excluded from the life God planned for them. But Jesus desires the opposite for you. He said in John 10:10, "The thief comes only to steal, and kill, and destroy; I came that they might have life, and might have [it] abundantly." Jesus wants each of us to have an abundant life with Him, not to be excluded from or denied it. But you must accept that it has to be on His terms, not yours. You have to listen to what He says and what His plan is. If you reject that, can you really expect Him to provide you with any kind of abundant life?

Hearts of Stone

The frightening thing about rejecting God's plan is that it results in a hardening of your heart. You must understand, the Bible says that hearts are hardened when God's commands are rejected. Want some proof? Try reading about Pharaoh. He heard God's command through Moses, and each time he rejected it, his heart was made even harder. Even believers' hearts can be hardened when they hear the Word of God and don't react to it or believe it. Hard hearts distress Jesus (Mark 3:5), so when believers let their hearts become hardened, Jesus reproaches them for their own benefit, like in Mark 16:14, "Afterward he appeared unto the eleven as they sat at meat, and upbraided them with their unbelief and hardness of heart, because they believed not them which had seen him after he was risen." That's also why we are warned in Hebrews 3:7–8, "Therefore, just as the Holy Spirit says, 'Today if you hear His voice, do not harden your hearts.'"

This callousness and sensuality are frequently evidenced in your life by impurity and greediness. When hearts are hardened, they become "callous." That word means, "separated from an ability to feel." You will cease to feel any joy, pain, or grief and often become apathetic toward life and others. God created you to be a feeling person, to feel the warmth of love in friendship and marital intimacy, as well as to feel terrible about doing wrong. But when your heart is hardened against God, your ability to feel diminishes. A callous person, desiring to feel something, can begin to do extreme things just to feel something. These hurting folks often give "themselves over to sensuality, for the practice of every kind of impurity with greediness" (Eph. 4:19). Sensuality is often defined as "an unbridled and excess lust." Sensuality is doing impure things and doing them with an intense "covetousness," which literally means, "a greedy desire to have more."

When a person hardens their heart against God, they routinely extinguish any ability to feel. Thus, many folks will go to any extreme to try and feel something—anything—and end up ruining their lives and the lives of others around them. This is a prime example of why so many people in our society are looking for satisfaction through the recreational use and abuse of drugs, self-mutilation, outrageous dress and behavior, through licentious sex, and even participation in extreme sports and the vicarious participation of reality television. It is because of their need to feel. It is also why today's criminals commit so many sick and twisted crimes, and why so many things that cross our paths, ears, eyes and minds seems to be crossing the moral line. In today's generation it seems that it takes more and more shocking behavior to get a reaction from or make our society feel anything. Today, if you find yourself engaging in more extreme activities just to feel, it is time you turn to Jesus Christ, who will soften your heart, open your eyes, and give you the abundant life that was always planned for you.

Selah (Ground your gear, take time to pause and reflect.)

Paul has been telling you that you should "walk no longer just as the Gentiles also walk" (Eph. 4:17). He means, I believe, that you need to march to the beat of the heavenly drummer boy and not the seemingly rhythmic but out-of-beat cadence of the world's alternative yet deceptively attractive drummers. He goes on to describe those who walk as Gentiles walk, as those Christians who set their minds on what is inappropriate, whose understanding is darkened, are currently restricted from the life God desires for them, and ignorant of the glory and goodness of God. Their hearts are hardened and callous. They practice, all too frequently, to perfect their existence by indulging and are trying to find completion and a wholeness and satisfaction in the sensuality and impurity of their earthly and temporal environments. They constantly endeavor to satisfy their desires for a lifestyle of more and more material wealth. Since the mortal period of our lives pales in the light of eternity, this world's treasures have no monumental worth. Theirs is a craving caused by an emptiness that can never be fulfilled, except by committing their lives to and developing a personal relationship with the Lord Jesus Christ. Now if you'll stop your "goldbricking" and get back on duty, you'll see that Paul is now saying:

4:20–24 You Did Not Learn from Christ to Live this Way

> "But you did not learn Christ in this way, if indeed you have heard Him and have been taught in Him, just as truth is in Jesus, that, in reference to your former manner of life, you lay aside the old self, which is being corrupted in accordance with the lusts of deceit, and that you be renewed in the spirit of your mind, and put on the new self, which in the likeness of God has been created in righteousness and holiness of the truth." (Eph. 4:20–24)

Paul is saying here, "Although the Gentiles (those worldly folks you know) live like this, *you* did not learn Christ in this way. That may be the way people in the world who do not know God live, but you ought to know better." That would probably be enough encouragement, even if Paul had finished his sentence there, but he didn't stop there. He went on to use that dreaded two-letter word, "If."

The Dreaded "If"

The word "if" in Scripture can be a scary term, because it often asks, "Are you sure this truth applies to you?" It frequently says, "This statement doesn't apply to you unless you meet the following condition." It says in Ephesians 4:20–21, "You did not learn Christ in this way, if indeed you have heard Him and have been taught in Him." If you've really heard Christ, if you've really been taught how to live in Him, then it's true that you did not learn Christ in this way. This is one of the times when Paul uses that word "if" to say, "Look, I don't doubt that you're Christians, that is, 'if' you're living a Christian life." Usually nobody wants to hear that rationale, and many people want to deny it applies to them or give it their own interpretation. But for the sake of clarity, it is repeated many times. For example, in Hebrews 3:14, Paul says, "We have become partakers of Christ, if we hold fast the beginning of our assurance firm until the end." Hebrews 3:6 says, "Christ [was faithful] as a Son over His house whose house we are, if we hold fast our confidence and the boast of our hope firm until the end." Colossians 1:22–23 says, "To present you before Him holy and blameless and beyond reproach—if indeed you continue in the faith firmly established and steadfast, and not moved away from the hope of the gospel that you have heard." 1 Corinthians 15:2 says, "You are saved, if you hold fast the word, which I preached to you, unless you believed in vain." 1 John 2:3 says, "By this we know that we have come to know Him, if we keep His commandments." Yes my friends, as the sayings go, "The proof is certainly in the pudding," and, "Actions always speak louder than words." However you want to slice it or dice it, Salvation is something the Bible says requires evidence—not to earn it but certainly to exemplify it. New lives will produce new fruit. And a changed life is confirmation that you have truly met Jesus Christ. That's why Paul is hitting this subject so heavily: "You can't live like the Gentiles. You need to walk worthy of your calling." You've heard it before, and you'll hear it again, "If you want to talk the talk, then you got to walk the walk."

Laying Aside Your Old Self

Paul encourages you to throw out the old and bring in the new. Ephesians 4:22, 24 says, "Lay aside the old self…(And) put on the new self." The old self is your former lifestyle, the one you lived when you were lacking in your knowledge of God. That lifestyle must be put away and replaced. The laying aside of the old self is an interesting process, because it needs to be done daily, as you will soon see. On the one hand, it has already happened. It was accomplished the instant you were born again. That's why it is sometimes referred to in the past tense, like in Romans 6:6, "Knowing this, that our old self was crucified with [Him], that our body of sin might be done away with, that we should no longer be slaves to sin." And in Colossians 3:8–10, "But now you also, put them all aside: anger, wrath, malice, slander, [and] abusive speech from your mouth. Do not lie to one another, since you laid aside the old self with its [evil] practices, and have put on the new self who is being renewed."

These verses talk about the old self having been crucified and laid aside already. But they also tell you to be a slave to sin no longer and to put away these bad habits you might still exhibit, even if only occasionally. That is the present and future part of the process, the daily part, of laying aside the old self. It is just as Jesus said in Luke 9:23, "If anyone wishes to come after Me, let him deny himself, and take up his cross daily, and follow Me." You've got to deny yourselves daily because your old natural man is no slouch. He is always ready to resurrect himself, to come back to life, to rear his ugly head and surprise you with just how corrupt and deceitful he (we I'll include myself here, since it is appropriate) can be. You need to replace the natural man with the spiritual man frequently. If you really understand the Word, you know "frequently" translates to "daily" for most of us. Scripture tells us in Romans 13:14, "Put on the Lord Jesus Christ, and make no provision for the flesh in regard to [its] lusts." It is a constant battle, these minute-to-minute choices you make as to what self you will wear. Will you choose the old man or the new one? Will you choose to put on the nature of the Lord Jesus Christ or that of the world?

Be Regenerated in the Spirit of Your Mind

The key to crucifying the old man daily is to make sure you're continually improving your mind by the Spirit. That means bombarding your conscious mind with good things, not the run-of-the-mill things of the world. Paul gives you good advice on this principle in Philippians 4:8 when he says, "Finally, brethren, whatever is true, whatever is honorable, whatever is right, whatever is pure, whatever is lovely, whatever is of good repute, if there is any excellence and if anything worthy of praise, let your mind dwell on these things." Too many people, including myself, allow their minds to be force-fed by the garbage barrage the world assails us with today. The visual stimulation of television all too frequently overflows with fraudulent lifestyles that amplify the things in life that are contrary to God's desires and intentions. The acoustic stimulation of today's music (if you want to call it that), as well as its violent and depraved lyrics, are degrading, embarrassing, and humiliating to many of us. The morals we're being persuaded by the world to accept as societal norms are tarnishing our witness. You've got to start filtering your mind's input and focus on things that are righteous. When you feed your mind a steady diet of things that are holy and spiritual, your mind will continue to be renewed. Paul commands you to do just that in Romans 12:2, "Do not be conformed to this world, but be transformed by the renewing of your mind." The word "renewed," as used here, literally means, "to be like the recently born." You need to get back to a childlike innocence like you were first born with and to renew your mind so that you will be as fresh and pure as a newborn child. You are told in 2 Corinthians 4:16, "Though our outer man is decaying; yet our inner man is being renewed day by day." May we truly become a nation of people who pray like David in Psalm 51:10, "Create in me a clean heart, O God; and renew a right spirit within me" (KJV).

Selah (Ground your gear, take time to pause and reflect.)

You have just finished learning from Paul that you need to lay aside your old life and start living a new Spirit-filled life. Now, as we tackle verse 25, he is going to tell us, "Because you need to be renewed in the spirit of your mind, you also need to be walking in the righteousness and holiness of the truth." So let's mount up again and learn a leadership lesson about integrity.

4:25 Speak the Truth

"Therefore, laying aside falsehood, SPEAK TRUTH EACH ONE OF YOU WITH HIS NEIGHBOR, for we are members of one another." (Eph. 4:25)

So, troops, you realize this means no more lying, right? Only the truth shall you speak. Yet lies and prevarications seem to be such an integral part of life for so many of us, don't they? Little falsehoods like, "I couldn't make it, I was sick," or "Nobody ever told me." How about, "I never said that about you," or, "I didn't know you wanted that done too." I can almost—I said almost—understand why honesty is so rare in the world, but I really have trouble understanding why it is so seemingly unknown among those who've been called to be righteous. It is, I believe, all about our deteriorating faithfulness. Remember when David cried out in Psalm 12:1–2, "Help, Lord, for the godly man ceases to be, for the faithful disappear from among the sons of men. They speak falsehood to one another; with flattering lips and with a double heart they speak." He also sang in Psalm 40:4, "How blessed is the man who has made the LORD his trust, And has not turned to the proud, nor to those who lapse into falsehood." "Lapse into" means "to slip into." However, many people don't slip off the road of life that leads to Heaven. No, more frequently it was by driving hell-bent for leather into dishonesty, deviousness, and corruption. Once they leave the highway to Heaven, they are quickly stuck in the muck; there they settle. You are blessed when you choose to speak the truth, though you do need to remember to speak it with true love and compassion as your motivation.

4:26–27 Is There Ever Any Appropriate Anger?

> BE ANGRY, AND YET DO NOT SIN; do not let the sun go down on your anger, and do not give the Devil an opportunity..." (Eph. 4:26–27)

After Paul discusses lies, he brings up the subject of anger. Surprisingly enough, some Christians do not consider anger to always be a sin. When brought about by a righteous cause, they believe anger is an accepted, understandable and expected emotion. They point out that undoubtedly there are many things that make God angry, yet He is without sin. That may well be, but the truth is very seldom do you have such pure motives for your anger. Your anger is usually goaded because you didn't get your way or didn't get something you wanted; it is because people wouldn't give in to you, or you weren't getting the respect and attention that you were sure you deserved. James understood this fact very clearly and explained it in James 4:1–2 when he said, "What is the source of quarrels and conflicts among you? Is not the source your pleasures that wage war in your members? You lust and do not have; [so] you commit murder. And you are envious and cannot obtain; [so] you fight and quarrel." Yes, your anger generally stems from your own egocentric motives. But even on the occasion that your anger is righteous and justified, you will enter into sin if you react in an ungodly way. Paul also tells you that if you don't deal with your anger immediately, but allow it to simmer, it will fester and provide an opportunity for the Devil to intervene and make you bitter, unforgiving, and maybe even a bit unrepentant. This happens when you assume your self-righteous anger was deserved by those you targeted.

I may not be an expert on anger, but I deal with anger a lot, both my own and that of others. It is a sin that continues to plague my "natural man," one I have to continually crucify to prevent it's resurgence. If I didn't habitually repent and deal with anger, it would devour me, making me a callous and bitter person, an unforgiving man, and a completely ineffective witness for Jesus. Remember, the only person responsible for your anger is you and you alone. It would pay you to remember, though, that the person who controls your anger also controls your actions, and your actions are your testimony. You can ill afford to relinquish your testimony, for which you are ultimately responsible, to anyone lest it come back around and bite your backside. You need to realize that you may be the only Bible a person ever reads. What kind of sermon do you think they will they receive from the life you are currently living? Ask yourself this question, "Are you a 'do as I say' leader for Christ, or are you prepared to be a 'do as I do' leader?" It is always good to learn something from everything you hear, but I'll wager a dozen doughnuts that those who made a habit of practicing what they preached have to a great extent made a more indelible impression on your life.

4:28 Let He Who Steals Be Industrious Instead

> "He who steals must steal no longer; but rather he must labor, performing with his own hands what is good, so that he will have something to share with one who has need." (Eph. 4:28)

Next Paul provides some inspired advice on a subject with which I feel I have some direct experience. Work, Paul says, since laziness is a disgrace to God. It is a sin to sit and collect welfare and unemployment when you are still able to work. It's probably easy to read this and think, "Well, I often worked at least twelve hours a day. I must be completely justified as far as this point is concerned, and I can read this without feeling convicted." I know that would be an easy sin for me to commit. But when I read what Paul has to say about the proper motives for labor in Ephesians 4:28, "In order that he may have [something] to share with him who has need," then I feel the bite of conviction. (Oops, shame on egocentric me.) Do you know why God has given each of us the strength, energy, and intelligence to work? To share what we have with those who have needs.

To many of you that just doesn't seem fair, does it? "Whatever happened to be self-reliant and provide for yourself?" "Why should I work so hard for what I get and then allow others to mooch off my blood, sweat, and tears?" Be careful, I hear your "old man" grumbling out there, the one who isn't good at sharing. When I work hard to earn something, I sure don't always want to give it away, or even share it, lend it, or let someone sponge off me when they ought to be working as hard as I did. I start to feel like they need to go earn their own. Then I stop and realize that's not the Jesus lifestyle I am commanded to exemplify. Whenever you ask that now-famous question, "What Would Jesus Do?" you need to remember just what He taught. Luke 6:30–38 says:

"Give to everyone who asks of you, and whoever takes away what is yours, and do not demand it back. And just as you want people to treat you, treat them in the same way. And if you love those who love you, what credit is [that] to you? For even sinners love those who love them. And if you do good to those who do good to you, what credit is [that] to you? For even sinners do the same. And if you lend to those from whom you expect to receive, what credit is [that] to you? Even sinners lend to sinners, in order to receive back the same [amount.] But love your enemies, and do good, and lend, expecting nothing in return; and your reward will be great, and you will be sons of the Most High; for He Himself is kind to ungrateful and evil [men.] Be merciful, just as your Father is merciful. And do not judge and you will not be judged; and do not condemn, and you will not be condemned; and if you pardon, and you will be pardoned. Give, and it will be given to you; good measure, pressed down, shaken together, running over, they will pour into your lap. For by your standard of measure it will be measured to you in return."

When I contemplate the truth of this Scripture, I become conscious of just how selfish I can be and that I have no room to blow my own bugle about how many hours there are in my eight-day workweek. I can only pray, "Father, make me more like Your Son Jesus." By the way, I hope you remember there is only one complete and correct answer to WWJD. It is a rhetorical question whose answer is eternally "JWADTRT" (Jesus would always do the right thing).

4:29–32 Where the Tongue Leads the Heart and Mind Will Follow

"Let no unwholesome word proceed from your mouth, but only such a word as is good for edification according to the need of the moment, so that it will give grace to those who hear. Do not grieve the Holy Spirit of God, by whom you were sealed for the day of redemption. Let all bitterness and wrath and anger and clamor and slander be put away from you, along with all malice. Be kind to one another, tenderhearted, forgiving each other, just as God in Christ also has forgiven you." (Eph. 4:29–32)

As he brings this chapter to a close, Paul spotlights the way you should speak to one another. He advises you not to allow anything to come out of your mouths that doesn't edify another person and provide them grace. Still, it seems my mouth is always more prepared to tear down perceived facades and dispense justice. I am sure that whenever I do that, the Holy Spirit residing within me is deeply grieved. He desires that I speak kindly to and about people, forgiving them even when they wrong me, because that's what Jesus did for me and for you. He even forgave those who put him to death on Calvary's Cross. The Bible points out that though Jesus was put to death He was then raised up from the dead on the third day. That same God who lives today has also commanded in Acts 10:42–43 that you "preach to the people, and solemnly to testify that this is the One who has been appointed by God as Judge of the living and the dead. Of Him all the prophets bear witness that through His name everyone who believes in Him receives forgiveness of sins." Before you can really understand and forgive others for what they've done to you, you need to receive the peace, grace, and forgiveness from God for what you've done to Him.

Selah (Ground your gear, take time to pause and reflect.)

(And this time perform a real "Gut Check" too.)

Paul has just spoken sternly to the Ephesians and by Heavenly inference to you and I, about walking the Christian walk, telling us to speak the truth instead of falsehood, to deal with anger in a holy way, to work so that we have enough to cheerfully share, and to be careful to see that our speech is edifying and full of grace. He ends by reminding us about forgiveness, of that which we have received and that which we are expected to offer others. Have you really got what it takes to live your life as a true 'Soldier of Christ'? Can you get down in the trenches and defeat the ways of the world that are battling for control of your life? Are you willing to sacrifice for others in the service of Our

Lord and Savior? If you can answer those questions with a resounding amen, then pick up your burden for others and follow me into battle. But be prepared for conflict. Satan is not a foe to be trifled with; instead he is like a prowling lion, seeking to devour and destroy his enemies. He need not, nor will he, waste time on doing battle with any but the strong Christian soldier, for the weak, feeble, uncommitted, untrained, and ill-equipped will fall victim to their own self-centeredness or be blown away by his minions.

5

5:1 Imitators of God

"Therefore be imitators of God, as beloved children…" (Eph. 5:1)

If you're going to be honest, sharing, and grace-giving in speech, you need to try to be mimickers of God, who is your perfect role model. Many times in Christian counseling sessions, people have been told they need to be more like Jesus, but they frequently try to excuse or minimize their sin by replying, "Well, I'm not God, I'm just a man. I can't really be like Him, so why should I even try?" Man, that's a cop-out if I ever heard one, especially for a reputed Christian to say. If you'll notice, you're not called to be extraordinary, or to be God, you're only called to be, as it says in Ephesians 5:1, "imitators of God, as beloved children." I think you know most children take pride in trying to imitate their parents. I know that for nearly my entire childhood, I always wanted to be like my dad. Good or bad, he was my dad, and even though he is no longer living, he's still my dad. He was in the Marine Corps too, and I truly wanted to be a Marine my whole adolescent life. Dad was a jet engine mechanic and loved working with tools, and I wanted to do the same thing. I still enjoy working with tools, as a matter of fact, though not at the level of proficiency at which my dad was capable. He was also into baseball and bowling, and I imitated him in those areas as well. It is in this way that we are called to imitate or be like God, not as all-powerful beings worthy of worship—heavens no!—but simply as dearly loved children, who want to be just like their dad.

5:2 Walk in Love as You Are Loved

"...and walk in love, just as Christ also loved you and gave Himself up for an offering, a sacrifice and us to God as a fragrant aroma." (Eph. 5:2)

The one thing you had best never overlook when you reflect on the Lord is His sacrificial love. Because of the love of God for each of us, Jesus gave up everything: His position and His life. Remember what John 3:16 says, "For God so loved the world that He gave His only begotten Son." Romans 5:8 states, "God demonstrates His own love toward us, in that while we were yet sinners, Christ died for us." If you are going to honestly imitate the love of God, you must make every conceivable effort to have an agape love, one that puts others' needs before your own. Are you up to that challenge? Can you make that commitment? Come on soldier, Sound Off!!

5:3 Beware!

"But immorality or any impurity or greed must not even be named among you, as is proper among saints..." (Eph. 5:3)

I know what you're thinking; didn't Paul just cover these topics in recent verses? I'll bet you are wondering, "Why is he going over them again?" You're thinking, "I've got it, I've got it already!" But honestly, do you have a concrete understanding? I'm not sure about you, but there have been biblical themes on which I've heard sermon upon sermon on for years before the true meaning clearly got through to me, and I said, "Oh, gees. Why couldn't I get this before? Why didn't I identify this behavior as sinful in the past? Why didn't I do anything about changing this until now?" So, we are going to go over these thoughts again because, while it may seem like you just covered some of them, both God and Paul realize a majority of you haven't completely applied them to your lives yet, and they remain hopeful that today you will reach a cross-roads and experience a defining moment in your lives.

Immorality, Impurity, and Greed

The Greek word for "immorality" used here is pronounced '*por-NI-ah.*" It doesn't take a valedictorian to figure out what words in our language are derived from it. It refers to any sexual activity outside of that occurring between a man and woman bound in marriage. This is an area of our lives that has been under vicious attack by Satan for a long, long time. His efforts can be readily observed throughout our modern society. We have worked hard as a culture to create a huge "gray area," while reducing the clearly defined "black-and-white" areas of morality to almost nonexistent territories. The hedonistic desires of the natural man are ravenous and prone to seek instant gratification as the primary solution to any carnal desire he may encounter. You tend to consider such temporal satisfaction as your right, and you know how you feel about your rights in America. They are twice as important as any responsibility someone may remind you that you also have. Or so you prefer to think.

"Impurity" is exactly what it sounds like, anything that is not pure and clean.

Impurity will defile your physical flesh (Gal. 5:19), your mind, and even your conscience (Titus 1:15).

Then there is "greed," which is a word you've looked at recently as well. It can be most accurately defined as "a gluttonous desire to possess more," whether it is directed toward money or any other self-designated idol with which you may be seeking to find fulfillment.

Not Even to Be Spoken About

Paul admonishes that these three things, immorality, impurity, and greed, are not to, as he says, "even be named among you." (Eph 5:3) The Greek word Paul uses here means "to utter or to make mention of the name." There is an important point here that Christians need to understand. You're not just commanded biblically to refrain from involvement with these things, but you are further warned not to even talk about them. Somehow you've been conned into thinking that you can see it, read about it, discuss it, and joke about it, as long as you're not guilty of doing it. But remember, Paul said to you earlier in Ephesians 4:29, "Let no unwholesome word proceed from your mouth, but only such [a word] as is good for edification according to the need [of the moment,] that it may give grace to those who hear." Next he will be telling us what unwholesome words are, and he'll get even more specific. So let's make a wake, all ahead full and try reading these next several verses and think about them for a moment.

5:4–7 Speech Befitting neither Man nor Beast

"…and there must be no filthiness and silly talk, or coarse jesting, which are not fitting, but rather giving of thanks. For this you know with certainty, that no immoral or impure person or covetous man, who is an idolater, has an inheritance in the kingdom of Christ and God. Let no one deceive you with empty words, for because of these things the wrath of God comes upon the sons of disobedience. Therefore do not be partakers with them…' (Eph. 5:4–7)

Three kinds of speech inappropriate for the Christian to exercise are discussed here as well as one constructive type. Let's take the negative first so we can culminate on a positive note, shall we? The word "filthiness" implies anything spoken that is of an "obscene, dishonoring, or shameful" character. You need to remember your mother's sage advice that I am sure she told you when you were just a child, "If you can't say anything nice about someone, then don't say anything about them at all." The Greek word for "silly talk" is from the same root as our contemporary word "moron." It is frequently translated "fool." You know from reading and studying the Bible that a fool is a person who lives as if there were no God and no tomorrow. No God and no tomorrow, now that is foolish!

"Silly talk," is the kind of talk that is used to speak impiously or irreverently. Much of this type of language is in use today because of the desensitization of the American public. Everyone is an expert at the use of double-meaning statements smothered with innuendo. When they are confronted about their language, I hear a great many people saying, "It's just a figure of speech." Well, my friend, "hellfire" is not just a figure of speech, and if a lot of people don't watch where their "silly tongues" are leading them, they will be in for a rude awakening when Satan springs his ambush.

Last on the negative list is "coarse jesting." It means anything that is disrespectfully humorous. The current term might be "put-down" or "cut-down." As Christians, our duty is to edify or build up people and their lives as we build Christ's Church. So I ask you to pay considerable attention to what comes out of your mouth. There should be no unwholesome language, no scoffing, mockery, disrespectful or deriding words, no egotism, no bragging, and no disgraceful or discourteous speech. Let your actions speak for you; they usually make a more lasting and truthful impression. As things begin to change in your life, the things that are not of the Holy Spirit will become incongruous, and you will feel discomfort when their presence is detected.

The one positive type of speech Paul mentions is always beneficial, so I'll reinforce it one more time before we press on. Use only edifying and grace-filled words, please! How about simply giving thanks? I still remember as a young Christian hearing the advice of wiser elders who taught me, "Where the tongue leads, the heart will follow."

No Inheritance in the Kingdom

What do you think happens to those who think it is OK to joke about these kinds of things, or who routinely employ them in their lifestyles? The hard and fast fact of the matter is that people who engage in such activities are riding on a runaway train to hell. Someday they will be experiencing the full wrath of God. Is that funny? I, for one, don't think so. Some people, who are still ostensibly living in the fleshly manner of the natural man, are laughing at the Christian way of life. To them it may seem meaningless or of little consequence. However, as Christians, your spirits should be terribly grieved for them. I must admit that the more God continues to work on me in this area, the more uncomfortable I become even being around this kind of speech and humor. My advice to you is like Paul's: Let's not be partnered with those in the world who are laughing themselves straight toward the shores of Gehenna. Remember, it's not a time-share resort.

5:8–10 Out of Darkness

> "...for you were formerly darkness, but now you are Light in the Lord; walk as children of Light (for the fruit of the Light consists in all goodness and righteousness and truth), trying to learn what is pleasing to the Lord." (Eph. 5:8–10)

Once you commit your life to Jesus Christ, you're no longer among those who travel in the darkness of the world. Christians are called "Children of God" and "Children of light." You possess an inner light and reflect the Light of Jesus, Our Lord and Savior. You are directed in Matthew 5:16 to "let your light shine before men in such a way that they may see your good works, and glorify your Father who is in heaven." That illumination is the fruit of the Spirit showing through, shining in all goodness and righteousness and truth. Therefore do not focus your minds on the latest insensitive comment, put-down, or one-liner, but instead concentrate on learning and doing that, which is pleasing to the Lord.

Selah (Ground your gear, take time to pause and reflect.)

OK, can we take a break for a moment and think about what the key points are in Paul's dialogue on the subject of our Christian walk.

He wants you to realize how you should, as Christians, interact with other people. Your actions should demonstrate humility, gentleness, patience, forbearance, love, unity, peace, sharing, kindness, and forgiveness. Wow! Can you imagine the impact that you would have on the world if you could exploit all the power you have through Christ for His kingdom and purposes? Another thing he is concerned with is how you should be occupying your time, and with what. You know deep within you should be serving the Body of Christ, earning a living, and doing such things as are pleasing to God. But what should you be saying to and about one another? You should understand by this point that Christians must always be speaking the truth in love, saying things that edify and give grace, not being participants in impious joking or discussing things that are unwholesome, immoral, or untrue.

I recognize some of you folks may be having a hard time with all of this. You might be saying, "This sounds too much like religion, and I don't want or need religion. What I need and want is a relationship with God. I believe in grace, and I don't need a Christian life that is full of legalism and works-based rules." My initial reaction to that response is that real relationships always take into account the other person's likes and dislikes. For example, if you truly love your spouse and you care what he or she honestly thinks, you consciously—and wisely so, will most likely—try to avoid doing the things he or she doesn't want you to do, and you try to do the things that bring him or her pleasure. Is there anything religious or legalistic about that? If you want to be in a right relationship with God, then He wants you to avoid certain things and do certain other things. Just don't forget His warnings, which occur all throughout the Scriptures and remind those who do the opposite that they have relinquished their birthright in God's kingdom. The way I see things, paying heed to these instructions in Scripture would certainly seem to do us no harm and would be more apt to benefit us.

5:11–13 God Is Not Night-Blind

"Do not participate in the unfruitful deeds of darkness, but instead even expose them; for it is disgraceful even to speak of the things, which are done by them in secret. But all things become visible when they are exposed by the light, for everything that becomes visible is light." (Eph. 5:11–13)

Jesus often refers to the good things you do as your fruits. These fruits can be produced through your repentance (Matt. 3:8), increased understanding of the Word (Matt. 13:23) and grace (Col. 1:6), dying to self (John 12:24), abiding in Christ (John 15:5), walking in the Spirit (Gal 5:22), and living righteously (Phil. 1:11). On the other hand, your being preoccupied with the things of the world often brings about unfruitfulness, things like worry, money, and materialism (Mark 4:19). Very little good comes from focusing your life on this kind of materialistic flotsam and jetsam. The Bible makes two easily understood statements regarding your fruits. The first, in Romans 7:4, says that Jesus Christ "was raised from the dead, that we might bear fruit for God." The second, in Luke 3:9, tells us that anyone who "does not bear good fruit is cut down and thrown into the fire." Can you now understand why Paul is so emphatic about your having nothing to do with the unfruitful deeds of darkness? Besides, do you really think God can't see in the darkness? Those deeds you do in the secrecy of darkness may remain hidden from the prying eyes of men, but nothing, absolutely nothing, will escape the omniscient, all-seeing eyes of The Creator. I used to tell the troops I trained, "If you aren't proud enough of what you choose to do to see it in the headlines of *The New York Times* tomorrow morning or watch it on the evening news with both of your parents tonight, then maybe you should reconsider your decision." Now consider Christ standing right beside you in front of the Father's throne answering for those fruitless deeds you've amassed. No, God isn't night-blind; He knows even those things you wish He didn't. Maybe you need to break out your own night-vision goggles and avoid those darkened pitfalls and other snares the Devil has laid out along the pathways of your lives.

Don't Speak of Them, Expose Them

I am sure you have heard it said many times, and we have even addressed the fact earlier in this study, that many Christians who would never consider committing certain specific sins have no problem at all wasting their time talking about those same sins. This is dishonorable behavior, especially for a soldier of Christ. We need to "lay it on the line." These are the weapons of the standard-bearers of darkness. When someone begins to joke about adultery, pornography, sorcery, or homosexuality (to name a few), they initiate the process of desensitizing people's hearts. When this desensitization sets in, how long can the societal moral norm remain unaffected? As a Christian, you need to expose this for what it really is. Paul's words to the Corinthians are a great reminder of this responsibility, and it's a great place to get started. Paul warns Christians in 1 Corinthians 6:9–10, and brother if you don't think this warning applies today, then you haven't read a newspaper, heard a radio talk show, or seen a movie in years. Look at what Paul says will be in our foe's arsenal of deception: "Do not be deceived; neither fornicators, nor idolaters, nor adulterers, nor effeminate, nor homosexuals, nor thieves, nor [the] covetous, nor drunkards, nor revilers, nor swindlers, shall inherit the kingdom of God."

5:14 It Says

> "For this reason it says, "Awake, sleeper, and arise from the dead, and Christ will shine on you." (Eph. 5:14)

Here Paul is making reference to what might have been an early Christian song or a cliché generally known to early believers. He is reminding them of the reason the phrase was coined. It clearly implies "Wake up. You're in the dark, but the light of the Word of God is all around you. If you will only wake up, you will see without a doubt how God wants you to live." If you think about all of the catch phrases we have today, like "What Would Jesus Do?" and the lyrics to so many hymns and praise choruses that we believers memorize, when I stop to think, it never ceases to amaze me how few Christians really listen to, understand, and apply the meanings of these sayings to their lives. I can just imagine Paul being so aggravated as his contemporary Christians were singing, "Awake, sleeper, And arise from the dead, and Christ will shine on you," while their actions exemplified the fact that they had little or no interest in speaking to those sleepers living among them who were still dead to Christ. In fact, I think he actually felt some of them were actually singing in their sleep themselves.

5:15–16 Walk Wisely and Make Good Use of Your Time

"Therefore, be careful how you walk, not as unwise men but as wise, making the most of your time, because the days are evil." (Eph. 5:15–16)

When I served in Vietnam in the 1960s, the most important man on any of our patrols was our point man. If the rest of the patrol was to avoid being surprised by the enemy or stumbling into booby traps, punji pits, or improvised explosive devices our enemy constantly laid out in our path to hinder our activities, the point man had to be a well-trained and observant person in whom we could have genuine faith. The man walking point had to observe and assess everything, miss nothing, recognizing when even the smallest thing was not as it should be. There was never a moment on patrol when he could "get lazy" or "goof-off." If he did, then any of the rest of us might have paid the ultimate price for his deficit. It is interesting, too, that the point man was frequently not the leader of the patrol. That should come as no surprise to anyone who remembers Jesus telling the disciples when they were arguing about rank and privilege at the Last Supper, that the least shall be the most important.

It is no different in spiritual warfare. In order to avoid the snares and pitfalls encountered on the spiritual battlefield, you need to be wary of how you walk, what you say and do, how you act and react, and how you spend your time. Let me tell you, I've gotten a lot of flack over the years for how much time I have wasted not doing the things I should have been doing. Frankly, watching two hours of TV probably isn't always sinful in and of itself, depending on what was showing on the "one-eyed babysitter," but was this making the *best use* of my time? Was this the *best* way I could have spent those two hours? No, I am sure it was not, and I have been tried and at times found wanting. Take heart, soldier. If I can still learn at my age, then there is still time for you to improve as well. Paul admonishes you in 1 Corinthians 10:23, "All things are lawful, but not all things are profitable. All things are lawful, but not all things edify." Sure, there will be *some* time you can devote to this or that seemingly harmless diversion, but should it be all the time? New Year's Day is coming (I started writing this in October), and no doubt many people will watch a few hours of football. No problem there, but does it profit and edify you to spend hours and hours, week after week, in front of the TV? Make sure that enough of your schedule is devoted to making the most of your time with God. The fact is, these days are truly evil, and many people are easily deceived about how busy they really are. I think it's their self-centered priorities that keep them busy.

5:17–18 Be Filled with the Spirit

> "So then do not be foolish, but understand what the will of the Lord is. And do not get drunk with wine, for that is dissipation, but be filled with the Spirit…" (Eph. 5:17–18)

I am the product of an alcohol-damaged childhood, and as such I've had a big chip on my shoulder about alcohol use and abuse for many years, but today I still strive to keep a biblical perspective on its use. It is clear to me that the Scriptures do not forbid the moderate and judicious consumption of alcohol for the average person, and I have personally consumed alcohol on occasion. In fact, if I am to continue in honesty, I must admit that during my transition from adolescence to adulthood, during my early military career in Vietnam, I tended to respond to the world's view of the use of alcohol more readily than I did to the Spirit's view. I was still in "Spiritual Boot Camp," though you'd have thought I pictured myself as a "Christian General."

The Bible does, however, emphatically counsel us, "Do not get drunk ever! To do so is sinful, and those who continue to overindulge in it shall not inherit the kingdom of God." If that sounds absolute and ominous, it is, but it's not me passing judgment, it is God's Word documented in 1 Corinthians 6:10, Galatians 5:21, and 1 Peter 4:3. When you over consume alcohol and establish it as a lifestyle, you turn over your thoughts, inhibitions, and subsequent actions to the forces of your natural and debased man. What license do you really think the "old man" is going to take as he seeks to satisfy his carnal desires? As long as you understand what the will of the Lord is according to His Word, you will avoid this kind of foolishness. But just in case you are asking, "How do I know what the will of God is?" I will tell you now that when the Spirit dwells within you and you are truly Spirit-filled, He will lead you and direct your thoughts and actions in accordance with the Scriptures, for that which is good and profitable.

5:19–20 Singing with Your Heart to the Lord

> "…speaking to one another in psalms and hymns and spiritual songs, singing and making melody with your heart to the Lord;

always giving thanks for all things in the name of our Lord Jesus Christ to God, even the Father..." (Eph. 5:19–20)

I am always singing the songs we sing in church and pray that they become a part of my whole life, providing me with thoughts on which to meditate, giving me a bearing for my prayer life, and helping me to worship the Lord. He deserves all your thanks. I pray that today and every day is a day of absolute thanksgiving, and that you will be thinking of your blessings and singing with your heart to the Lord about the many reasons He is worthy of your thanksgiving and praise. In fact, why not make every day a day of "thanks giving?"

Selah (Ground your gear, take time to pause and reflect.)

Paul has been telling us to ensure that our relationships with other Christians are godly, and I will add that there is no more important relationship between two warriors than the understanding of teamwork. A true warrior is one who will sacrificially lay down his life for his comrade-in-arms, not foolishly, but as a last resort for the benefit of his fellow soldier. Nowhere else can Christians experience and exemplify this type of relationship better than in the relationship between a husband and wife. So while you review the things you have learned so far, in the light of your marriage, you need to stand by for a lesson in love, submission, and teamwork.

5:21 Be Subject to One Another

"...and be subject to one another in the fear of Christ." (Eph. 5:21)

Although many men like to start reading at verse 22, where the wife's role is outlined, the proper beginning is really verse 21. The word "subject" or "submit" is defined as "to cooperate, making yourself lower." In every relationship, someone has to subjugate him or herself; otherwise any difference of opinion would result in conflict because no two people can be unanimous in every one of their opinions and desires. This positioning is not done simply by virtue of authority or power but out of humility and respect. When you are told to fear the Lord, it is an admonition to respect His position and authority, just as your children are directed to "fear" or "respect" you as parents. It is important to realize that submission and subjection have nothing to do with who is the most qualified to make the decision. Even at age twelve, Jesus had wisdom and power far beyond His earthly parents, Mary and Joseph. But as it says in Luke 2:51, "He continued in subjection to them." Governmental authorities sometimes make ridiculous decisions, but the Bible says in Romans 13:1, "Let every person be in subjection to the governing authorities." There are times that you know better than your boss, (I often wonder if I am the only one who has ever felt this way) and yet the Scriptural command in Titus 2:9 is, "[Urge] bond slaves to be subject to their own masters in everything, to be well-pleasing, not argumentative."

Husbands and wives, subjection to one another is not an issue of "I'm right, you're wrong, so you need to surrender." It is an issue of mutual compassion, peace, and respect. Ephesians 4:2–3 says, "With all humility and gentleness, with patience, showing forbearance to one another in love, being diligent to preserve the unity of the Spirit in the bond of peace." Is winning the argument more important than keeping peace? Is getting your way worth losing unity? To quote my daughter, "Hello! I think not." But neither is being able to control one another. Accomplishing harmony is going to take some work on each person's part. Just remember, Paul told the Philippians, "I can do all things through Christ who strengthens me."

5:22–24 Wives

"Wives, be subject to your own husbands, as to the Lord. For the husband is the head of the wife, as Christ also is the head of the church, He Himself being the Savior of the body. But as the church is subject to Christ, so also the wives ought to be to their husbands in everything." (Eph. 5:22–24)

Ladies, bear with me for a few minutes. I promise to take myself and other males to task shortly. In any relationship, someone has to have the ultimate authority and have the final say when a unified agreement cannot be reached. In the case of a marriage, God has appointed the man. Ladies, I am sure you will agree it's not because we are more intelligent, more discerning, or more spiritual, but only by virtue of our order of creation. 1 Corinthians 11:8–9 says, "For man does not originate from woman, but woman from man; for indeed man was not created for the woman's sake, but woman for the man's sake." Of course, when it comes to our relationship to God, we are both created equal, as we are told in Galatians 3:28, "There is neither male nor female; for you are all one in Christ Jesus." Ultimately, however, the line of authority that God established in marriage places the husband as the head of the wife.

Men, you need to accept this position with a bit of awe and trepidation, for God has also told you, "For to whom much is given, much is expected," and, "Those in authority will be held to a higher standard." (Luke 12:48) If you have a hard time dealing with that, I don't blame you. But that isn't going to change a thing; it's just like when God appointed the Levites as the priests of Israel. Certainly there were other godly people among the tribes, and without a doubt there were some real bad apples in the tribe of Levi. But God set things up that way, and when Saul, from the tribe of Benjamin, stepped into the role of priest, God dealt harshly with his egocentric decision. God appointed Moses and 250 leaders as the authorities over the people of Israel, not because they were better than the rest but plain and simply because God had chosen them. When Korah stood against them, saying in Number 16:3, "All the congregation are holy, every one of them, and the LORD is in their midst; so why do you exalt yourselves above the assembly of the LORD?" He rebelled against God's chosen authorities; the ground opened up and swallowed him.

You can plainly see it has nothing to do with qualifications. It is merely about whom God chooses. Rebellion against God-appointed authority is always judged. Romans 13:1–2 says, "Every person is to be in subjection to the governing authorities. For there is no authority except from God, and those, which exist, are established by God. Therefore whoever resists authority has opposed the ordinance of God; and they who have opposed will receive condemnation upon themselves." God has chosen the husband to be the authority. Should a wife refuse to believe or practice this command to esteem her husband higher than herself, she shall be judged for rebellion. Worse yet, she blasphemes (the Greek word is pronounced *blas-fay-MEH-o)* the Bible. Titus 2:5 says, "Being subject to their own husbands, that the word of God may not be dishonored." So, in spite of the fact that your husband may not deserve your submission and in spite of the fact that he might be so ungodly that it seems impossible to submit to him, when you submit, you free God's hand to work on him. 1 Peter 3:1–2 says, "In the same way, you wives, be submissive to your own husbands so that even if any [of them] are disobedient to the word, they may be won without a word by the behavior of their wives, as they observe your chaste and respectful behavior." I credit a great deal of my Christian growth to my wife, who, in spite of my frequent stupidity and thickheadedness, has submitted without (or with very little) complaint to many of my decisions. In doing so, she freed God's hand to thump my head!

5:25–33 Husbands

> "Husbands, love your wives, just as Christ also loved the church and gave Himself up for her, so that He might sanctify her, having cleansed her by the washing of water with the word, that He might present to Himself the church in all her glory, having no spot or wrinkle or any such thing; but that she would be holy and blameless. So husbands ought also to love their own wives as their own bodies. He who loves his own wife loves himself; for no one ever hated his own flesh, but nourishes and cherishes it, just as Christ also does the church, because we are members of His body. FOR THIS REASON A MAN SHALL LEAVE HIS FATHER AND MOTHER AND SHALL BE JOINED TO HIS WIFE, AND THE TWO SHALL BECOME ONE FLESH. This mystery is great; but I am speaking with reference to Christ and the church. Nevertheless, each individual among you also is to love his own wife even as himself, and the wife must see to it that she respects her husband." (Eph. 5:25–33)

Ah yes, as I promised ladies, now for the husbands. Far too many dumb husbands I have encountered in both of my uniformed careers have lorded it over their wives by adhering only to the part of the Scripture that says, "You have to submit to me." Guys, before you even think you have the right to demand that she perform within her job description, you'd better do two things. First, recall just who wrote hers. Second, make sure that you're performing within yours. Take a minute and reread your responsibility in Matthew 7:1–5. Now that you have reread what your job description is, do you really understand it? "Yeah, I just gotta love her." Do you really believe that? I hope you got more than that out of that passage. These verses go to abnormal lengths to define what kind of love you ought to be showing toward her. It is the same type of love that Christ demonstrated to the Church: agape love, a completely selfless, giving, sacrificial kind of love that makes you empty yourself of all your pride, let go of your position, and refuse to demand your rights. Philippians 2:5–8 says:

"Have this attitude in yourselves which was also in Christ Jesus, who, although He existed in the form of God, did not regard equality with God a thing to be grasped, but emptied Himself, taking the form of a bond-servant, [and] being made in the likeness of men. And being found in appearance as a man, He humbled Himself by becoming obedient to the point of death."

This is the kind of love we're talking about. Husbands, let's take a little test. Can you say each of the below statements to your wife right now?

- "I love you like Christ does."

- "I will sacrifice my own life, position, and desires for your sake."

- "I will cleanse you with the Word of God by reading and explaining it to you."

- "I will love you just as much as I love myself."

- "I will nourish you and cherish you forever."

If you have a problem saying all of those things honestly, then you'd better not be running around like a crazy man shouting the battle cry, "Submit, woman, submit!" And if you can honestly say all of those things, you likely wouldn't dream of bandying about the phrase, "Submit, woman!" Because if Jesus is truly your example, then you will want to imitate how he demanded submission in Mark 8:34, "And He summoned the multitude with His disciples, and said to them, 'If anyone wishes to come after Me, let him deny himself, and take up his Cross, and follow Me.'" Realizing the great responsibility you have been awarded, do you really want to say, "If anyone wants to follow me, you are welcome to come with me? I'm heading down the road of God's will, and I'd love you to tag along with me and if you don't want to follow right now, I'll just keep marching down that path of God's will anyway." After all, God tells us in 1 John 4:19, "We love, because He first loved us," and in Romans 5:8, "God demonstrates His own love toward us, in that while we were yet sinners, Christ died for us." So just keep on loving and dying to self, regardless of the response you get. Don't let a lack of response influence you. Colossians 3:19 says, "Husbands, love your wives, and do not be embittered against them." Just keep on loving God, loving your wife, and loving those around you.

The Mystery

Paul's final point on this topic is that marriage is a mystery, which is from the Greek word pronounced *"moos-TAY-ree-on"*. It can be defined as something hidden or secret. Yet the open secret of marriage is that it is a living picture of Christ and the Church. You are to love one another just as Christ loves you, unconditionally and sacrificially, and you must willingly submit to each other as you submit to His authority. Your relationship with each other is one of the most observable sermons that can be preached. I pray that you are communicating it as you should be.

Selah (Ground your gear, take time to pause and reflect.)

We have investigated thus far in Ephesians many things regarding the importance of the Christians' relationships with others. We just finished looking at the relationship of husbands and wives, a great example of the unity of the Church. Now you must prepare yourselves to look at some other relationship basics. So "Fall in!" Do I have your undivided attention? Ladies? Gentlemen? Then at a gallop, Forward Yo-o-o!

6

6:1 Children, Obey Your Parents

"Children, obey your parents in the Lord, for this is right..." (Eph. 6:1)

It shouldn't be a surprise to anyone with kids that this is probably one of the first verses many people teach their children. I can think back and recall many times when one of my own wonderful children was just a tad disobedient; they would be standing there, either receiving a lecture or anticipating punishment, and I would remind them with a paraphrase, I'm sure, of Ephesians 6:1, "Children, obey your parents in the Lord, for this is right." Have you ever thought about it carefully? I mean, why do you think children obey their parents? It really is a simple question, though it is often difficult to answer. They should obey their parents because it's right! It's the proper thing for all children to do, and Christian children in particular. As time progresses, I have experienced that obedience to authority of any type seems to be occurring less and less frequently. In public places, I have seen children of all ages blatantly telling their parents "No!" when given a simple command. I have seen children become animated, vocal, and quite insubordinate with their fathers and even physically violent with their mothers, challenging their parents to get their own way.

I could not conceivably imagine this happening back in the days of my childhood, when *Father Knows Best* was more than a television show. But the Bible has provided us with a warning that it would happen. Do you recall when Paul told Timothy in 2 Timothy 3:2–4 that in the last days, people would be "lovers of self...revilers, disobedient to parents, ungrateful...unloving, irreconcilable...without self-control...reckless, conceited, lovers of pleasure rather than lovers of God." Doesn't this sound like today's headlines, or maybe something straight off the *Jerry Springer Show?* Yes, Christian children should obey their parents because it is the right thing to do in the Lord. They shouldn't need any help from Dr. Phil or any other person, and you, as parents, must recognize when your children start indicating an unproductive desire for pleasure over their love for God. The application of fair, consistent, and loving discipline (remember the origin and definition of this word, it has the same root as "disciple" and means to teach and not to punish) is a biblical mandate that you as parents have been given and must adhere to if you want to see your children grow up to be the kind of people God desires them to become. Proverbs 19:18 says, "Discipline your son while there is hope, and do not desire his death."

6:2–3 Honor Who? Why?

"Honor your father and mother (which is the first commandment with a promise), so that it may be well with you, and that you may live long on the earth." (Eph. 6:2–3)

Where on earth did Paul come up with that? He must have smoked some bad crack! Those might well be the comments heard around many a U.S. high school and even some of the middle schools I have spent time in as an adult. But the source of Paul's advice is not really of this world, for Paul is quoting from the Ten Commandments, and you all know who the author is, don't you? "Honor your father and your mother." In Hebrew, the Lord used the word pronounced *"kaw-BAD"*, which is "to give weight to." But he is speaking to the Ephesians in Greek and chooses to use their word, pronounced *"tim-AH-o"*, which literally means "to approximate their value as precious." You might think that these two verses are continuations of the previous one referring to children and that I am only talking to those who are under eighteen. Sorry to burst your bubble, but there are many folks over eighteen who still have issues with their parents. How do you get along with your parents? Have you spoken to either or both of them recently? Maybe you have a strained relationship, or you feel you have a good reason to not respect them as you should. OK, now think about the example you're role modeling in your relationship with your mom and dad. Have you predetermined their value as precious? What are they really worth to you?

I never got a real chance to know my mother because she died when I was five years old, and my father was a combat-hardened Marine who spent his life after Mom's death trying to find something to fill the void that was created in his life and, sadly enough, I don't think anyone ever took the time to introduce him to the Lord until he was too casehardened to respond. No, my dad went from marriage to marriage and booze to loneliness then back again without ever finding the peace that God wants for all of his children. I could never break through that veneer he had built around himself to keep from being hurt by others. That veneer was an albatross to me in that it kept him from show-ing me the love I think he felt for me. Living in that environment, I could eas-ily have become a bitter and hardened soul, if not for the intervention of God through the influence and impact of certain individuals and Christian families he placed in my life. From them I learned to look at the "half-full glass" and not at the "half-empty glass." As a result of God's divine intervention, today I still consider my mother and father precious. They are among the most influ-ential people I have ever known, though sometimes for the things I learned were harmful, and not for the things I learned that were good. I still respect them as human beings and honor their memories as my parents, without whom I would not be here today.

Not everyone can view his or her mom and dad that way. But whoever your parents were or are, whatever mistakes they made raising you, whatever real or perceived difficulties they created for you, or even if they failed to give you the love you needed, this Scripture commands you to restore their value as prized and invaluable, for unless you do, things will not go well for you. You may not even live long on the earth. Job pointed out that the bitter soul longs for death (Job 3:20–21), and that is a true statement, even if you don't want to admit it. Begin today to highly regard your mom and dad and think of them as pre-cious. This is the hour to repent for any malice and unforgiveness you may be harboring. Let go of any hurt and anger that still separates you from the total and perfect peace God wants you to experience. I don't want to overlook those of you who were blessed with God-fearing Christian parents who brought you up in a loving, Christ-centered environment. How great it would be if we all could experience such joy. Even still, I have observed blessed children who on occasion seem to forget the admonition of Paul to revere their parents. Don't give Satan a foothold on the battleground of family relationships. Respect your mother and father for who they are, not for what they have done.

6:4 Do Not Provoke, but Discipline

"Fathers, do not provoke your children to anger, but bring them up
in the discipline and instruction of the Lord." (Eph. 6:4)

As a father, I have read this verse many times, and I will admit it can be a
little bit confusing at first glance. It seems like a natural phenomenon that if
you refuse to give into your child's every request, they will eventually get upset.
Does this mean you are provoking them to wrath or anger? I really don't think
that was what Paul had in mind. As I have studied, I found my belief vindi-
cated. Over the years, I have read numerous and diverse commentaries, all of
which were biblically grounded in their basic interpretation and application.
Now the proverbial light bulb gets illuminated, or as my daughter was fond of
saying at one time, "Hello, is someone finally at home up there?" My efforts at
understanding this concept have at last revealed that Paul has answered this
for you! The word "but" (or "instead" as it is translated in the New Interna-
tional Version (NIV) tells us that the solution is also being offered. Ephesians
6:4 says, "But bring them up in the discipline and instruction of the Lord." By
bringing your children up with ungodly discipline and instruction, you would
unquestionably be provoking them to wrath. Children whose fathers punish
them out of anger, unfairly, with brutality, or arbitrarily, will be justifiably
goaded into a rage. The word "instruction" here literally means "to place in the
mind an understanding." Fathers who by example place ungodly principles in
their children's minds are predestining them to a life of trouble and sorrow.
Fathers, are you training up your children in the way they should go, so that as
adults they shall not depart from those ways, and doing it in a godly way?
Does anything need to change in your home and in your relationship with
your children? Are you living a sermon worthy of repeating?

6:5–9 The Subordinate and Commander Relationship

"Slaves, be obedient to those who are your masters according to the
flesh, with fear and trembling, in the sincerity of your heart, as to
Christ; not by way of eye service, as men-pleasers, but as slaves of
Christ, doing the will of God from the heart. With good will render
service, as to the Lord, and not to men, knowing that whatever good
thing each one does, this he will receive back from the Lord,
whether slave or free. And masters, do the same things to them, and

give up threatening, knowing that both their Master and yours is in heaven, and there is no partiality with Him." (Eph. 6:5–9)

I once looked at this superficially during a study of Colossians. However, there are some critical points being dealt with here in Ephesians that it will definitely benefit us to investigate before we complete our mission.

In the Sincerity of Your Heart

When Paul directs subordinates to obey their masters, he doesn't mean for it to be a reluctant, fear-induced kind of obedience. He says in Ephesians 6:5 that the obedience is to be "in the sincerity of your heart, as to Christ." There have been many times in my life in both my careers when I have been guilty of obeying on the surface, while inwardly lacking any semblance of genuineness. That is not the sincerity of heart that God requires of us. If any relationship is properly grounded in Christ and His Word, authenticity will be appropriately embedded.

Eye Candy

He also says that your obedience is not to be eyewash. This means your dedicated service must not only be performed when a commander is watching but always. I am sure there are times for some of you that, even when the Captain is watching, your compliance is only grudgingly given. This kind of attitude is suggestive of the Venus Fly Trap, a plant that is sweet and flattering on the surface but deadly underneath. This insincere type of servant attitude will never fool anyone for long and will always come back to haunt you. You would do well to remember what wise men already know: that flattery is like perfume, it's meant to be sniffed not swallowed, a lesson I am sure your superiors have already learned.

Your Commander in Heaven

In a nutshell, it makes no difference what your duty or station is in life, whether you are a child, parent, boss, or employee, God is calling you to be like Him in all your relationships. May all of your thoughts and deeds be glorifying to Him, whether at home, at school, at work, or at play.

Selah (Ground your gear, take time to pause and reflect.)

Now Paul says, "Finally." This word in the biblical Greek means "what is remaining or the rest of it." So, after five-and-a-half chapters of marching through Ephesians, Paul is at last telling us, "This is the last of it, this is the end of what I have left to say to you." On a somewhat humorous note, Paul is like many pastors I have heard speak. Even though he has identified this as his last point, it is so jam-packed with information that it could take us quite some time to analyze what he has to say in his closing admonitions. Well, troops, you are in the final phase of basic training. It will soon be time to issue you your spiritual 782 gear, but not before you learn what its intended use is, and you get up-close and personal training with the equipment itself. So grab your PT gear, and let's break a sweat! It is just about time to get physical with the Devil.

6:10–13 Be Strong in the Might of the Lord

> "Finally, be strong in the Lord and in the strength of His might. Put on the full armor of God, so that you will be able to stand firm against the schemes of the Devil. For our struggle is not against flesh and blood, but against the rulers, against the powers, against the world forces of this darkness, against the spiritual forces of wickedness in the heavenly places. Therefore, take up the full armor of God, so that you will be able to resist in the evil day, and having done everything, to stand firm." (Eph. 6:10–13)

Paul's exhortation to be strong in the Lord identifies the means you have available, which enables you to have the strength to stand against the Devil's attacks. That strength is identified as being both in the Lord and from the Lord. That strength is the only way you can ever truly experience what Paul understood when he told the Philippians, "I can do all things through Him who strengthens me" (Phil. 4:13). That strength is readily available to all believers, but it is only acquired by getting into the *full armor of God*.

What Constitutes Our "Full Armor Issue"

When I joined the U.S. Marine Corps in May of 1963, the first combat equipment I received was referred to as "782 gear," sometimes shortened by "salty" veterans to "duce gear." These nicknames were birthed by the form that was used to hand receipt this "armor" to each individual Marine (You U.S.

Army vets will remember it as your TA-50). Well, you can believe me, it seemed like there was a ton of it, and I felt sure David must have felt the same way when Saul offered him his armor to wear into battle against Goliath. I wondered just how I was supposed to conduct operations in the field against a mobile enemy force when I was so encumbered with all this protective equipment. Well, fear not, the full armor of God is not physical armor that you strap onto your possibly "out-of-combat-shape" body. Actually, it is more effective for your personal and spiritual protection than any amount of metal or Kevlar (I happily wore vests of this material for years as a peace officer) could ever be. I want you to remember as we get into this topic, protective armor is made primarily to increase your chances of survival when you are under attack. Consider, for example, a baseball player's helmet; it is designed to cover the head and the ear exposed to the opposing team's pitcher, or my law enforcement bulletproof vest that was designed to prevent fatal wounds inflicted by gunshots to the upper body. Another example would be a knight's armor that was designed to protect him from arrows, swords, maces, and lances. Armor is designed to address the anticipated method of attack or threat that you are most likely to encounter.

Therefore, the full armor of God has been designed by Him to provide you with the ultimate protection from even the most unwavering attacks of our spiritual archenemy, the Devil, and his forces.

Understanding Spiritual Skirmishers

Your soul's real enemies are not human beings. They are spiritual beings, and yet they are very, very real. Paul told you on more that one occasion that you struggle against powers and principalities and not against the forces of this world. Your enemies are the Devil and his legions of demonic forces. I realize some of you may have a problem with this concept and will endeavor to express your contempt at its validity by saying, "How can you believe in that stuff? I don't put any faith in anything I can't see." OK, so let's look at a few things I can't see but still believe exist. I cannot hear radio waves without a radio, but they must be there all around us. I cannot see ultraviolet (UV) light, yet UV rays give me sunburn. I cannot see the air and wind, but stick your hand out the window of a moving car and you'll learn how airplanes fly. As for the air itself, try breathing in a vacuum. It looks the same, but I doubt seriously that you'll last very long. Though I cannot see the spiritual realm, the Bible is very concerned with making sure you understand that there definitely are battles that you cannot see going on beyond the realms of your limited understanding.

Take, for example, the following story from 2 Kings 6. There was a time when war had broken out between the nation of Aram and Israel. Since the Lord was on Israel's side, God kept telling Elisha about all the secret plans that the king of Aram was making. There could have been no better intelligence provided. The king of Aram believed that he had a traitor in the midst of his command, feeding information back to the Israelis. However, his people insisted that it was Elisha the prophet, so the king decided to capture him. One night, he sent the Aramean Army to surround the city of *"DO-thawn"* (no, no, not Dothan, Alabama, the home of the U.S. Army's flight training program—You see, we are not going to get to fly on our own until our life here on earth is over), where Elisha was staying. 2 Kings 6:15–17 says:

> "Now when the attendant of the man of God had risen early and gone out, behold, an army with horses and chariots was circling the city. And his servant said to him, "Alas, my master! What shall we do?" So he answered, "Do not fear, for those who are with us are more than those who are with them." Then Elisha prayed and said, "O LORD, I pray, open his eyes that he may see." And the LORD opened the servant's eyes, and he saw; and behold, the mountain was full of horses and chariots of fire all around Elisha."

This passage reveals that there are spiritual beings that exist beyond the physical limitations of your sight and hearing. Many of these beings are evil, exclusively devoted to fulfilling the Devil's desire for control of our lives. Satan's purpose is, as John 10:10 says, "only to steal and kill and destroy," using any method he can to accomplish this goal.

The Devil's Operational Plans (Oplans)

It is extremely important to be aware of and understand the crafty wiles of the Devil. 2 Corinthians 2:11 says, "In order that no advantage be taken of us by Satan; for we are not ignorant of his schemes." It is a well-known military adage that the best way to defeat or defend against your enemy is to know and understand him and his motives as well or better than you understand your own. You must never remain ignorant of how he operates, or he will always gain the advantage over you. The Bible says Lucifer is a very crafty foe (Gen.

3:1). Fortunately for us, he has only a limited number of schemes in his reper-toire. When you read Genesis 3, you will find out that he tries to make you question what God's Word says (Gen. 3:1), and He tries to get you to believe that God's Word isn't completely true (Gen. 3:4). Then He will try to make you think that you can be—to steal a Hollywood film title—the *Master and Commander* of your own life (Gen. 3:5). He will also attempt to convince you to do things that are motivated by pride and by an ego-based desire for earthly recognition. He knows you have a natural deep-seated desire for three distinct needs: affection, recognition, and a sense of belonging to something larger than yourself.

The Devil is a professional when it comes to exploiting your most minus-cule flaws. Remember when he whispered in King David's ear, "Wow—look how big your kingdom has gotten! I wonder how many people you govern?" 1 Chronicles 21:1 recounts that "Satan stood up against Israel and moved David to number Israel." The Devil will also afflict you in order to get you to curse God. Look what he did to Job. He destroyed all of Job's possessions and had his sons and daughters killed. Then he afflicted him physically, telling God in Job 1:11, "Touch all that he has; he will surely curse Thee to Thy face." And lastly, the Devil is the accuser of all the brethren (Rev. 12; Zech. 3). He will readily point out your sins and flaws as well as those of your fellow Christian soldiers, trying to make you feel overwhelmed, weak, worthless, and vulnera-ble. This is using ad hominem logic, both circumstantial and abusive, which infers he is giving up on attacking the argument you are using about God's love, and he's going directly after you. Imagine him saying, "OK, so God really cares about people and wants them to be His children; He loves them—them, yes, but not you. Christ could never forgive you for all those atrocious sins you've committed. You're the perfect paradigm of a lost cause!"

Stand Fast, Soldier

All of these are schemes that the Devil has devised and these are the plans, which he follows. They can be very effective, dangerous, and deadly. But now that you are aware of them, the Holy Spirit is urging me to help you organize an effective defense, so you can stand firm against his efforts, rendering them futile. That defense plan has already been designed for you. It is accomplished by using the full armor God has provided you. We will spend the rest of this document examining this armor in great detail: the belt of truth, the breastplate of righteousness, the boots of the Gospel, the shield of faith, the helmet of salvation, and the sword of the Spirit.

But as we get to it, I'll issue my last warning to you. As you go through this basic training with "your spiritual duce gear," make this training count. I mean really personalize it. It is not enough just to know about it. You must practice with it and use it. To my knowledge, a Kevlar vest in the trunk of a police cruiser never saved a single officer's life. When young David volunteered to face the giant Goliath, King Saul wanted to make sure that David was well-equipped. 1 Samuel 17:38–39 says, "Then Saul clothed David with his garments and put a bronze helmet on his head, and he clothed him with armor. David girded his sword over his armor and tried to walk, for he had not tested [them]. So David said to Saul, 'I cannot go with these, for I have not tested [them].'" But you see, wearing Saul's armor wasn't going to do David any good because it didn't fit him. David was not familiar with it, nor had he tested or trained with it. He just wasn't used to it. So I don't want you to wait until you are engaged in the midst of a spiritual mêlée before realizing that you need to take your armor from the trunk of your car!

I remember hearing a story about a husband and wife who were standing outside of the Sanford Stadium at the University of Georgia on the day Georgia was to play Tennessee. The husband said, "Bummer! I wish I'd brought the piano with us." His wife replied, "The piano? Why on earth would you want to bring our piano all the way from Valdosta to Athens to a football game?" The husband said, "Because I left the tickets for the game on it!"

Put on the full armor of God and practice with it faithfully, and you will be equipped to stand firm against the attacks of our common enemy, Satan.

Selah (Ground your gear, take time to pause and reflect.)

The Apostle Paul has just issued a "FragO" (Fragmentary Order) directing you to put on the full armor of God so that you can stand fast and resist the assaults of the Devil. Beginning with this segment, you will be spending your next six training assemblies becoming proficient with the six pieces of armor Paul lists, one article at a time. I suggest you consider the following statements carefully as you resume going through your spiritual basic training. First, you will not need armor if you never go into battle. Second, you will never go into battle if you never join the army. Third, you will surely go into battle if you join this army, for God's enemies have vowed to fight until the last man is defeated. Fourth, you have been issued five times more defensive equipment than you have offensive equipment, so you are very well-protected. Fifth, all the armor you are issued is designed to be worn primarily as protection for your front because God does not expect you to turn your back and retreat during a conflict. Sixth, but certainly not least, you will need to be familiar with, train conscientiously with, and become extremely proficient with the only offensive weapon God has provided you: the sword of Truth—the Word of God. Now soldier, it's time to "lock and load and rock and roll."

6:14a Having Girded Your Loins

"Stand firm therefore, *having girded your loins with truth...*" (Eph. 6:14a, italics added for emphasis)

No, I didn't say girdled, I said "girded." Now there's a word you don't hear much in today's society. However, it was not uncommon in biblical times. For example, after King Herod had killed James, he arrested Peter. One night, when Peter was "catching a few winks" in jail, an angel appeared in his cell. Acts 12:7–8 says, "And he struck Peter's side and woke him up, saying, 'Get up quickly.' And his chains fell off his hands. And the angel said to him, 'Gird yourself and put on your sandals.'" "Gird yourself," means to tie up or wrap up your loose garments in your belt. Remember, during biblical times men wore loose apparel such as robes, togas, and skirts of various lengths, just as many Arabs do today. If you anticipated that you might be required to fight, run, or move quickly, you would, as was the vernacular of the day, "gird your loins," or gather the billowing parts of your garment into your belt. This was done to keep you from tripping over or having your movements obstructed by your billowing attire. Jesus used this same Greek word for girding, pronounced *"per-id-ZONE-noo-mee"*, when He told His disciples in Luke 12:35, "Be dressed in readiness, and keep your lamps lit." Having "girded your loins" can be understood to mean to be dressed in readiness, ready to move, or unhindered.

The Only Genuine Truth

I need to give you a definition of truth to guide you before I go much further. This seems difficult to do today, because today truth doesn't appear to have a common meaning to everyone. "My truth may not be truth to you, and neither my truth nor your truth may contain an ounce of real truth." One of the times Jesus appeared before Pilate, while the Governor of Judea was interrogating Him, Jesus told him that He had come to testify of the truth. John 18:38 says, "Pilate said to Him, 'What is truth?' And when he had said this, he [Pilate] went out again." In case you might be interested in finding out what the answer was that Pilate didn't stick around for, the Bible makes it readily accessible. The defining statement is found in Romans 3:4, "Let God be found true, though every man be found a liar." God will always be found true, for He is truth. Consequently, everything He speaks is truth, which means the Gospel is the truth; indeed the entire Bible is the truth. It is repeatedly called "the Word of Truth." Psalms 119:142, 151, and 160 say, "Your law is truth…all Your commandments are truth…The sum of Your word is truth…" Jesus said He is the truth in John 14:6, and the Holy Spirit is truth. Everything about God is truth. Today we live in a time, when a person cannot depend on very many things to be absolute. This is primarily because of our penchant to be overly tolerant even to the point of corruption; it is very inspiring to have the concrete knowledge available that God is always truth.

Man's Lack of Veracity

Man, on the other hand, is not a truthful being. (Ouch! That hurt, because I was appropriately even including myself). The Bible informs us that all men engage in, and often even try to perfect, many practices that actually oppose truth. These include lying, insincerity, hypocrisy, partiality, unrighteousness, prejudice, fallibility, and deception. Mankind apparently does not care much about the definition of truth and continually does things with the definition of truth and the application of truth. Here are few examples: "exchanged the truth"(Rom. 1:25), "do not obey the truth" (Rom. 2:8), "did not believe the truth" (2 Thess. 2:12), "gone astray from the truth" (2 Tim. 2:18), "oppose the truth" (2 Tim. 3:8),"turn away their ears from the truth" (2 Tim. 4:4),"turn away from the truth" (Titus 1:14), "lie against the truth" (James 3:14), and "lie and do not practice the truth" (1 John 1:6).

Your First General Order: Use and Preach Only the Truth

In case you have forgotten, a "General Order" is not an order for or from a General. It is an order, or command if you prefer, that applies to the entire membership of the organization. In our case, it applies to every Christian soldier. It is to be anticipated that this particular question will arise among some of you trainees: "If the truth is so unfamiliar to man, how will he ever be able to discern it?" Well, if you think about it for a moment, I'm sure you can come up with the answer. The Church is supposed to be the world's preeminent sustainer of the truth. Paul called the Church, "the church of the living God, the pillar and support of the truth" (1 Tim. 3:15). Unfortunately, though, sometimes the Church has fallen a bit short. Without a doubt, this generation has not seen the Church constantly supporting the truth. Dishonest televangelists, deceptive miracle-hawkers, and a plague of sexual immorality and subsequent cover-ups have all characterized at least part of the Church as not supporting the truth. You must never lack the courage, however, to stand up and insist that the Church return to being a pillar and supporter of the truth.

Whenever any member of the law enforcement profession seemingly falls from grace, all of the other peace officers I know feel the sting of betrayal. But we all draw on our own personal moral courage and continue to stand up for our ideals and convictions and hold on to the ethical standards we swore to uphold. Similarly, when Peter and Barnabas were hanging out with the Gentiles, they were representing the truth accurately. But when some of the Jews from Jerusalem observed them doing this, they came to them, accusing them of wrongdoing by this association. This had an adverse affect on Peter and Barnabas, and they began to act hypocritically and withdrew from the Gentile believers. Paul took umbrage with this and feeling a bit "righteously indignant" with them, got in their faces and said, that they were not straightforward about the truth of the Gospel (Gal. 2:14).

Yes, friend, the truth must be accurately preached and correctly represented in the Church, with neither partiality nor error. As it was said of Jesus in Mark 12:14, "Teacher, we know that You are truthful and defer to no one; for You are not partial to any, but teach the way of God in truth." You, too, can never afford to compromise the least bit on the truth, especially for the sake of personal or political expediency, personal gain, reputation, partiality, or even your own well-being, because your God "desires all men to be saved and to come to the knowledge of the truth" (1 Tim. 2:4).

Having Girded Your Loins with the Cartridge Belt of Truth

And so, as you look at the scenario Paul is drafting, each Christian is a soldier should gird his or her loins with the truth. It should be quite obvious that heeding his words will enable the truth to keep you from being tripped up in your Christian walk while you're running the (rat) race of life. You must never forget that there is a lot more to the saying, You know the maxim I'm talking about, I'm sure, It goes like this, "You shall know the truth, and the truth shall set you free," than most people seem to understand. Yes, free of the quagmire of falsehoods and deceit that often make matters worse in the lives of so many of you who struggle in the everyday ambushes you run into with your enemy, the Devil. The good thing about the truth is that since there is only one truth, you will have much less to remember than the person who must keep their lying and deceiving ways cataloged in order to keep from becoming entangled in the inevitable web of deception they created.

Proclaim Truth

Your Second General Order states that each Christian's life is to be distinctly recognizable by its truthfulness. Not only must you preach the truth, but it is also obligatory that you practice it. Now where did I first hear, "Practice what you preach?" I don't think I can even remember. I do know, though, that I'd rather see a sermon than hear one any day, or have someone go with me rather than merely tell me how to get somewhere. You need to be compassionate but truthful in all that you speak and do, for God commanded you in Zechariah 8:16, "These are the things, which you should do: speak the truth to one another." And in Colossians 3:9 we are commanded, "Do not lie to one another." God is so grievously offended when you quibble with the truth no matter what excuse you provide when you do it. Not only because we're misrepresenting Him, but also because we've completely disregarded Him just like He told us we would in Isaiah 57:11, "Of whom were you worried and fearful when you lied, and did not remember Me nor give Me a thought?" Try and remember this analogy regarding reasons and excuses when you make up your next excuse. A reason is like a bowl and an excuse is like a colander. A reason will hold truth as a bowl holds water, and truth flows out of an excuse like water flows out of a colander. There is another way to tell them apart. You make up a reason for doing something before you do it and an excuse after you do it, usually to get out of the trouble doing it got you into.

Exterior or Interior Truth

So why do some folks have so much trouble telling the truth? Before anyone can expect to really be truthful, the truth must first be applied to their own lives. You can't be honest with other people until you're really honest with yourself. You may not learn this in a psychology class, but you will definitely learn it from the Word of God. You are told you must first speak the truth in our hearts in (Psalm. 15:1–2). The Psalmist also wrote in Psalm 51:6, "Behold, You desire truth in the innermost being." The Lord knows that if you aren't girded with the truth, you'll be foundationless, unstable, and vulnerable to the schemes and persistent ambushes of your adversaries. Don't forget that knowing or memorizing these "general orders" regarding the truth will do absolutely no good unless you internalize them and they become your way of life. Many people go through basic training without ever having the principles of good military leadership imprinted on their character. These soldiers seldom last past their initial enlistment. Even the way they wear their uniform exemplifies their lack of total commitment for their profession. Don't ever become a "do as I say" leader, when with God's help, you can be a "do as I do" leader for Christ's glory and for your own deliverance.

Deceit Always Has its Consequences

Do you remember Ananias and Sapphira? They are explicit examples of people in the Church who didn't stand firm in the truth. They sold a piece of property and gave some of the money to the Church. But they weren't truthful about the amount they gave. Even though there was no requirement to do so, they pretended they were giving all of it. They were told in Acts 5:3–4, "Why has Satan filled your heart to lie to the Holy Spirit and to keep back some of the price of the land? While it remained unsold, did it not remain your own? And after it was sold, was it not under your control? Why is it that you have conceived this deed in your heart? You have not lied to men but to God." As a result, they paid the ultimate penalty when he and his wife fell over dead. They decided not to stand firmly in the truth but, desiring instead the praise and adoration of the world, concealed the truth from men—but not from God. Look what it cost them! Why did this happen? It happened because they hadn't girded their loins with the truth. Don't be deceived about the sinful lifestyle of not telling the truth. If you are starting to internalize the ways of the Lord and believe you are becoming a proper Christian soldier, then remember what John said, "If we say that we have fellowship with Him and yet walk in the darkness, we lie and do not practice the truth" (1 John 1:6). And so today, may your prayer be like David's in Psalm 86:11, "Teach me Your way, O LORD; I will walk in Your truth."

Selah (Ground your gear, take time to pause and reflect.)

While some of you taking this time to train with the Lord and I may currently be in basic training—being equipped to put on and to use the "full armor of God" for the first time so that you are able to stand firm against the attacks of the Devil. Others of you have already advanced to the next stage of your training, the SOI (School of Infantry) phase, or the AIT (Advanced Individual Training) phase, or maybe you are assigned to your first combat unit. Well, either way, you have just finished looking at the first piece of armor in your Issue: the importance of truth in your life. Your use of the truth keeps you from being entrapped in a lethal web of dishonesty. Now you will get an indication—in the second half of verse 14—of the importance of another item of spiritual protective equipment you have been issued. So, gird your loins and move out, smartly soldier, as the Evil One is on the move too.

6:14b The Breastplate of Righteousness

"...and having *put on the breastplate of righteousness...*" (Eph. 6:14b, italics added for emphasis)

Before you can understand this next piece of your armor, I need to be sure you know what a breastplate is. Since an actual breastplate is found today mainly in the historical military section of a museum, I'll describe it for you. It is a piece of armor that covered a soldier's body from the collarbone to the hips. Depending on what the solider could afford, it was either made of all leather or leather with metal accoutrements that primarily covered the front but sometimes included the back, or if it was made of a single solid piece of metal, it usually adorned only the front of the wearer's torso and often bore decorations. It was sometimes worn over a shirt of chain mail. Its chief purpose was to protect the soldier's vital organs in battle, principally the heart. The image Paul is creating is that righteousness acts like a breastplate in providing protection to the Christian warrior.

Using the Soldier as a Reference?

Many theological scribes wax eloquent when writing or speaking about how Paul, sitting in prison and chained between two guards, looked around and started drawing spiritual analogies vis-à-vis the armor his guards were wearing. If this had happened, it would be valid, as Jesus frequently used His surroundings to develop images and parables such as those in Matthew 6:28, "Observe how the lilies of the field grow; they do not toil nor do they spin," and in Matthew 10:29, "Are not two sparrows sold for a cent? And yet not one of them will fall to the ground apart from your Father." I don't think Paul would have been doing anything wrong, but neither do I believe that is from whence Paul's inspiration was derived. I believe that his inspiration came directly from God Himself. Remember, Peter told us in 2 Peter 1:21 that the Scriptures were written when "men moved by the Holy Spirit spoke from God," and God had used this same symbolic speech in expressing Himself before. In Isaiah 59:17, the Lord described Himself as having "put on righteousness like a breastplate, and a helmet of salvation on His head." I don't believe the illustrations of a breastplate of righteousness and a helmet of salvation used by Paul in Ephesians were conceived in a Roman prison; they originated in the heavenly realms of God.

Righteousness?

Do all types of righteousness act as a breastplate? Is there a special kind of righteousness Paul is talking about? To answer the second question first, positively yes, as there are several kinds of righteousness. First of all, you have self-righteousness. Do you ever, in fact, it is the most common type, and the righteousness I find folks to be the most familiar with. Of course, most people think they are never infected with this disease themselves, although they feel extremely qualified to spot it in others. The burden of self-righteousness is conceived and nurtured when people put their trust in performing what they conclude are good works in order to earn their salvation. Luke 18:9 describes these kinds of people as "people who trusted in themselves that they were righteous." By relying on their self-proclaimed righteousness and trusting their own behavior to be better than that of the vast majority of others, they are confident they will be on the eligibility list for "heavenly tenancy." Sorry if I am about to "bust your bubble," but none of us is righteous on our own. The Bible makes that clear to us in Isaiah 64:6 when it says, "All our righteous deeds are like a filthy garment." Romans 3:10 tells us, "There is none righteous, no not one."

Another kind of righteousness is the righteousness that God has provided to you. This is Christ's righteousness that God sees us cloaked in because, as it says in 1 Corinthians 15:3, "Christ died for our sins." But this righteousness is not the type Paul would have had to encourage the Church to put on because we receive this righteousness when we are saved. Freeze right there, mister! Take a quick look back at Romans 3:22, "The righteousness of God (is available) through faith in Jesus Christ for all those who believe." Verse 13 infers that you are to "take to yourselves" the full armor of God and verse 14 tells you to "put it on." You did nothing to take or put on the righteousness of God when you accepted His leadership in your life. He freely gave it to you. Thus, the breastplate of righteousness Paul is referring to does not apply to either of the preceding types of righteousness—neither the righteousness of Christ by impartation nor your own self-righteousness for salvation—but in fact, to a personal righteousness, which you must put on for your protection.

Protected by Our Personal Righteousness?

Personal righteousness? You must think I just suffered a severe blow to my head without my helmet on. How can we, the unwashed, have any form of righteousness? Consider this if you will. The kind of righteousness Paul is talking about, I believe, is simply doing what is right, as is mentioned in Romans 12:17, "Respect what is right in the sight of all men." Your behavior, your witness, your speech, and your thoughts, indeed your public and private lives, need to be consistently righteous. Your lives are to be clearly discernable by their righteousness, and you are to be continually walking in it. Check out your next spiritual general order, which is found in Romans 6:13, "Do not go on presenting the members of your body to sin as instruments of unrighteous-ness; but present yourselves to God as those alive from the dead, and your members as instruments of righteousness to God." With righteousness as your breastplate, you will be protected from two types of attacks that could conceiv-ably put you out of action: the false and deadly accusations of the Devil and the desensitization or deterioration of your heart.

Damaging Accusations

You are warned in 1 Peter 5:8 that the Devil is on the prowl to devour you, and he will try to accomplish this by bringing vicious accusations against you, which are intended to destroy your witness and steal or weaken your confi-dence. He will cause people to malign you. So, as you are instructed, "Keep a good conscience so that in the thing in which you are slandered, those who revile your good behavior in Christ will be put to shame" (1 Pet. 3:16). Per-sonal righteousness, if worn and lived daily, will act as a breastplate of protec-tion against these attacks of the Devil. So listen up! Understand and live your life with integrity, knowing and showing what it really means to live "above reproach." Then you, as a Christian, will walk in righteousness, and when you do your life and testimony will not be subject to any damaging, truthful indict-ments.

The Desensitizing of the Heart

Another way in which righteousness acts as a breastplate of protection for the Christian is to guard your heart against becoming calloused and hardened. You must protect your heart. You are told in Proverbs 4:23, "Watch over your heart with all diligence." When you sink into sin, your Spirit is justifiably troubled. Your heart should condemn you and your actions. If it doesn't, see 1 John 3. Left unchecked, your heart can be hardened to the point where it leads to agnosticism or even atheism, destroying any relationship you may have established with God. It is because Job walked in righteousness that he was able to say in Job 27:6, "I hold fast my righteousness and will not let it go. My heart does not reproach any of my days." Living a life protected by righteousness will surely help defend your heart against deterioration. A Roman soldier would never dream of going into battle without his breastplate, nor a wise police officer work the "mean streets" of his or any community without wearing his bulletproof vest. Do you honestly consider it wise to ignore the breastplate of righteousness in the upcoming spiritual battles you will undoubtedly face?

Selah (Ground your gear, take time to pause and reflect.)

Paul has given the following insight in Ephesians 6:10–13:

> "Finally, be strong in the Lord and in the strength of His might. Put on the full armor of God, so that you will be able to stand firm against the schemes of the Devil. For our struggle is not against flesh and blood, but against the rulers, against the powers, against the world forces of this darkness, against the spiritual forces of wickedness in the heavenly places. Therefore, take up the full armor of God, so that you will be able to resist in the evil day, and having done everything, to stand firm."

The "full armor of God" as you are now aware, indicates that there are a number of items that make up the whole. Being familiar with all of them is necessary if they are to assist you in remaining strong as a Christian warrior who stands firm in battle and resists every foray the Devil launches against you. Your "spiritual kit" consists of six items. You have familiarized yourself with two of these items. You have learned what it means to be girded with truth and to put on the breastplate of righteousness. Now you are going to "train" with your third piece of biblical 782 gear: your "combat boots." So, as we used to say in "The Old Corps," "grab your 'utes' and grab your boots! You are definitely going to need them in combat.

6:15 Having Shod

> "and having shod *your feet with the preparation of the gospel of peace*..." (Eph. 6:15, italics added for emphasis)

One of the difficult aspects of reading our Bible or studying a commentary is having to add words to our frequently inadequate vocabulary. Having grown up traveling extensively and even having lived in many different locations around the United States, I have had ample opportunity to meet many people who have never heard the word "shod" used in conversation. Of course, in horse country there are many people who know the expression quite well, and "a well-shod horse," is not an uncommon phrase. As it turns out, according to my research and an English professor I know quite well, it is a Middle English word, the past participle of the verb "to shoe," and may be defined as meaning, "having put shoes on." The definition of the Greek phrase Paul uses here is analogous to that. It means "having tied or fastened to your feet."

"Our Combat Boots of the Gospel"

As he does here, Paul in several of his other writings (1 Cor. 9:7; Phil. 2:25; 2 Tim. 2:3–4, Philemon. 1:2) brings to his readers' minds with analogies the concept of the Christian as a soldier. In light of the current spiritual battlefield on which you are training and fighting, it appears his comparison has a great deal of legitimacy. You can easily accept, in this day and age, the idea of combat boots as being a soldier's standard footwear. However, in his day, soldiers' shoes were much like everyone else's. They were leather sandals, which were secured to the foot by lacings that wrapped up around the soldier's calf. The difference between the general public's sandal and a soldier's sandal was the hobnail pattern of metal studs or spikes that stuck out from the soles of the soldier's sandals. These studded soles provided both superior traction and more stable footing that enabled his rapid movement over rough terrain. I have been told that many historians acknowledge a huge part of Alexander the Great and Julius Caesar's wartime successes were due to the superior training and footwear of their soldiers. Paul is revealing to you the secret to standing firm: a secret that you must realize will require your "combat footwear" to be considered a vitally important part of that stability.

Training Required

Even though this is spiritual armor and you're not tying on real-life shoes, you are supposed to make certain your spiritual feet are "shod" with the preparation of the Gospel. The word for preparation used here comes from a Greek word pronounced *"het-oy-mas-EE-ah,"* which means readiness. The same kind of readiness of which Peter spoke when he said in 1 Peter 3:15, "But sanctify Christ as Lord in your hearts, always being ready to make a defense to everyone who asks you to give an account for the hope that is in you, yet with gentleness and reverence." Ready to give an account, ready and prepared to preach the Gospel of peace. Are you always ready with the Gospel when someone asks you about Christ? Are you well-trained and equipped to present it in a temperate, nonconfrontational, but uncompromising way? Are you outfitted and able to share it with reverence and complete accuracy out of your sense of duty, gratitude, and respect for God? Tragically, many of you are ill-prepared. You may have some of the elementary concepts down, but how many of you have really taken the time to become "shod" with more than the foundation of the Gospel of peace?

The Gospel of Peace

OK, so let's examine this Gospel then, shall we? And maybe you'll find out why it's called the Gospel of peace. As you should have committed to memory by now, the word "Gospel" means "good news," and not just any old good news. The good news you have all been called to proclaim is that although man's sin has made Him an enemy of God, God has offered him a means to declare a ceasefire and reconcile. The Bible makes it absolutely clear that every human being has made themselves God's enemy because of sin. Isaiah 59:2–3 says, "Your iniquities have made a separation between you and your God, and your sins have hidden His face from you so that He does not hear. For your hands are defiled with blood and your fingers with iniquity; your lips have spoken falsehood, your tongue mutters wickedness."

It makes no difference what your sins are, whether they're something you've said, something you haven't done, or something you have done; these sinful actions have separated you from God. But God doesn't want you to remain His enemy. He loves you copiously, and so He made the definitive and final sacrifice for your redemption and reunification. He decided to take the penalty of your sin upon Himself and make the ransom payment for you. That price was His death on the Cross. Romans 6:23 says, "For the wages of sin is death." Jesus Christ died in our place. Romans 4:25 says, "He was delivered over because of our transgressions." Romans 5:8 says, "God demonstrates His own love toward us, in that while we were yet sinners, Christ died for us." The Gospel of peace says that even though your sins have made you God's enemy, He has always offered to be your true friend by willingly accepting your penalty upon Himself. All you are required to do is believe that He did this and to display it by living with true faith, and you will have an unparalleled peace. You have been told in Romans 5:1, "Therefore, having been justified by faith, we have peace with God through our Lord Jesus Christ." And so the Bible continues in Romans 5:10, "While we were enemies, we were reconciled to God through the death of His Son."

This, my friend, is the Gospel of peace. You will need to be well-versed in it, or you won't be able to stand firm against the ill winds of evil that are bound to buffet your life. Though sharing the Gospel can be frightening and may seem like an unapproachable task, this feeling of trepidation often comes because you're unprepared and convinced that the great unwashed masses don't want to hear it. You are afraid people will be angry with you if you say anything to them about God. If I am really honest, I'm not so sure I was happy to hear His message when I first heard it either. It bothered me, offended me, and might have even made me angry, mainly because it convicted me. You see, I never felt guilty about anything until I met the Lord, but I also never felt truly good until I felt that guilt. You see, back then I had no reference for good or bad. Today, I'm so unbelievably happy that it was preached to me. It takes a lot of effort—effort that I am not capable of on my own—to worry about what God thinks about my actions more than what man thinks about them. I now understand what Isaiah meant in Isaiah 52:7, "How lovely on the mountains are the feet of him who brings good news, who announces peace and brings good news of happiness, who announces salvation."

Selah (Ground your gear, take time to pause and reflect.)

Up to now in your basic training, I have been talking about the preparation you've received so far in your study of the full armor of God. You have accumulated the following facts. First, you must be girded with truth. Second, you must wear your breastplate of righteousness. Third, you must have your feet shod with the Gospel. Now you will be introduced to the next piece of you armor: the all-important shield of faith.

6:16 The Shield of Faith

"...in addition to all, *taking up the shield of faith* with which you will be able to extinguish all the flaming arrows of the evil one." (Eph. 6:16, italics added for emphasis)

The shield of faith, just what kind of image does that conjure in your mind? The word Paul uses here for shield refers to the style Roman legionnaires used—large and four-cornered, a shield that a soldier could hide his entire body behind. Your shield of faith, when properly deployed, will protect you from "all the flaming arrows of the Evil One," whenever you take refuge behind it.

What Flaming Arrows?

Why are you in danger? Because as a soldier in Christ's Army, you are a dedicated enemy of the Evil One and in his arsenal he has many flaming arrows meant for your unconditional destruction. These are arrows of evil launched at you by an enemy who has no greater desire in his heart than to see you physically and spiritually dead. Your adversary, the Devil, opposes you so ardently that it will take a great deal of training and faith to withstand his onslaught.

The Bible describes the destructive nature of the Devil in numerous ways. John describes him as the red dragon, whose tail sweeps the stars from Heaven in Revelation 12:4; Peter describes him as a lion, prowling around seeking to find prey to devour in 1 Peter 5:8; Jesus called him a murderer and a thief in John 8:44 and 10:10; and here in Ephesians, Paul is equating him to an archer, launching fiery arrows of misfortune at you. These arrows get their Greek name from the verb meaning "to cast." So they really refer to something that is launched against you, such as missiles, arrows, darts, javelins, and spears. These fiery projectiles often take the form of hardships and temptations. Simon Peter said in 1 Peter 4:12, "Do not be surprised at the fiery ordeal among you, which comes upon you for your testing, as though some strange thing were happening to you." You should remember from Job: the Devil's objective is to destroy you (or any of us) by putting you through ordeals of defeat and distress, hoping that you'll lose your faith (your shield), curse God, turn away from Him, and head rapidly down hell's freeway toward certain death and destruction. This tried-and-true technique frequently works because the only thing that stands between any of you and complete failure is this shield of faith you can hide behind. If you or I lose that shield, the Devil's blazing arrows will surely prove fatal. But if you maintain that faith, you can use your shield to smother his fiery arrows.

The Faith

It seems to me that a vital and important part of Christian life would be missing without a good understanding of what faith is, how to get it, and how to use it. An element of your basic training should contain some instruction about faith. A classic example of this theme is Hebrews 11, which lists a number of historical Bible personalities who had great victories in their lives against all odds because of their unfaltering faith. It says in Hebrews 10:38–11:1, "But my righteous one shall live by faith; and if he shrinks back, my soul has no pleasure in him. But we are not of those who shrink back to destruction, but of those who have faith to the preserving of the soul."

"Now faith is the assurance of things hoped for, the conviction of things not seen.." (Heb 11:1) When you recoil or retreat from difficult situations as a Christian soldier, it appears to observers that you have thrown away your shield of faith. Throwing down your shield will very likely lead to your destruction. If you maintain your faith, however, it will indeed shield you. Now let's determine just what constitutes faith. In my opinion it's a concrete assertion and unyielding belief in what you cannot see. I can't see air, microwaves, or sound waves, but I believe beyond any shadow of a doubt they exist. Is this belief the faith that will shield me from the Devil's sizzling arrows? It is not. The Bible says that the indispensable faith required for our protection is faith in God (Mark 11:22), in Jesus (Acts 3:16; 20:21; 24:24), and in His blood (Rom 3:25). You are told in 2 Thessalonians 2:13, "This is the truth, which will shield you, save you, and sanctify you." Though I haven't actually seen God physically, my faith assures me that He exists and lives both in the world and in my heart today. Yes, you heard me right; I serve a risen Savior. What good would it do to put my faith in a Savior who wasn't in this world of chaos and walking beside me every day? We may not see Him protecting us, but my faith gives me complete certainty that He is doing and will continue to do just that. You may never have a "legal document" in the palm of your hand stating you belong to God and have established your citizenship in Heaven, but you should recognize by faith alone that it is absolutely and positively true.

Fluctuating Faith

Now, faith is not an "on or off," "yes or no" or "one or zero" thing. It exists in different intensities and is frequently, though not appropriately so, dependent on circumstances. The strength of your faith may depend on how well your life is going at the time and the depth of your relationship with Christ, if one even exists. There are many biblical examples of how faith can affect you; the following are but a few: you can be full of faith (Acts 11:24), you can be lacking in faith (1 Thess. 3:10), you can be strong in faith (Rom. 4:20), you can be weak in faith (Rom. 4:19), you can continue in the faith (Acts 14:22), or you can turn away from the faith (Acts 13:8). No matter how you view it, your faith will be a part of your life and your witness for Christ as a positive or negative example.

Modest Faith

Are you one of those people who recurrently find themselves on the low end of the faith scale? You might be the type of person who says, "Brother Ray, I just don't have that much faith." Are you always questioning your faith? Do you feel that weakened faith is having an adverse affect on your witness? First of all, let me assure you that you're certainly not the first to feel this way, nor are you by yourself. When Jesus was telling the apostles to be on their guard in Luke 17:5, the apostles begged the Lord to increase their faith. They knew faith could grow. Paul saw it happen to the Thessalonians, and he wrote to tell them how encouraging it was to see it in 2 Thessalonians 1:3: "Your faith is greatly enlarged." So you are in luck because even if you have weak faith, it can be increased right now, wherever you are, just by the exhortation, amalgamation, and edification of the truth of the Word of God. For a good start, read Romans 10:17: "So faith comes from hearing, and hearing by the word of Christ." Remember that Paul and Barnabas traveled to several cities, strengthening the souls of the disciples, encouraging them to continue in the faith, and saying, "Through many tribulations we must enter the kingdom of God" (Acts 14:22). Don't fret; everyone needs to be reminded that these difficult times and tribulations should never be allowed to rob you of your faith. Your shield of faith is the only thing you have to extinguish the fiery darts and arrows of Satan and his minions!

Selah (Ground your gear, take time to pause and reflect.)

Just as a reminder, during your last four training assemblies, I've been discussing your spiritual basic training. You have been receiving training on each of the pieces of the full armor of God, which I have described as your spiritual "782 gear." Equipment the Lord God Almighty issued you, the master of all armor makers. You should have gleaned from your prior training what it means to have your loins girded with truth, to put on your breastplate of "personal" righteousness, to have your feet shod with the Gospel of peace, and to take up your shield of faith. It is time now to scrutinize the final defensive piece of armor you are to be issued: your helmet of salvation.

6:17a Your Helmet of Salvation

"...And take *the helmet of salvation*..." (Eph. 6:17a, italics added for emphasis)

Helmets really shouldn't need much explanation, should they? It matters not if it is a soldier's helmet, a motorcyclist's, a bicyclist's, a hockey player's, or a pilot's, you know what a helmet is designed to do. Its purpose is to protect your head and everything it contains! Though, in my case, I've often been told that it would probably not seem like a helmet would be protecting very much.

What is Salvation?

While you know what a helmet is, your perception of salvation may not be as concrete. "Salvation" is one of those words that gets bandied about a lot in religious dialogue but is not wholly comprehended. Salvation is a noun (remember back in elementary school you learned that a noun is a person, place, or thing). It is what you receive when you're saved. For example, when someone rescues you from drowning, they have literally saved you from death. So what you have received from this rescuer can be referred to, in a way, as salvation. Likewise, if you are involved in a traffic accident and the police, emergency medical technicians, and the emergency room staff save you, you could honestly say they all contributed to your salvation. In Christianity, people refer a lot to being saved, and speak often about receiving salvation. In these cases, they're not talking about a physical occurrence; they're talking about being saved from, well from, aaaahh—from what? That's what most people seem to get confused about when discussing salvation. The Bible says that when you confess Jesus as your savior you are saved from all sorts of things that could destroy you. Simon Peter told the Israelites in Acts 2:40 that they needed to "be saved from this perverse generation!" If you immerse yourself too deeply in the practices of any of the generations of today, you do so risking death from the inside out. Do you recall when Paul told the Thessalonians that people who don't receive salvation are dying in their wickedness? It was in 2 Thessalonians 2:10. If you become obsessed with wickedness, death will devour you from the inside out.

Regardless of the circumstances surrounding how or why you die in sin, you will in due course be required to stand tall before God. His wrath will then be poured out upon you. It is for this reason—if not for many others—that salvation is so utterly indispensable to you. It is only with salvation that "we shall be saved from the wrath of God" (Rom. 5:9). It is essential that you remember when you receive salvation that God becomes "the source of eternal salvation" (Heb. 5:9). Salvation is so encompassing that the Bible reminds Christians often that they have been saved, are being saved, and shall be saved. If you are a Christian, (and if you are not, then why aren't you? Can you really build a case for not being one?) you have been saved from this perverse generation and will not die condemned by your sins. Nor will you be required to incur the incalculable wrath of God.

The Helmet of Salvation

OK, it is time to draw this metaphor into a more precise focus. How can salvation be linked in any way, shape, or form to a helmet? Well, when people mull over the possible meanings for this piece of the full armor of God, it will rarely dawn on them that it is not really salvation that is the helmet. First and foremost, Paul is writing to Christians and directing them to "take up" the full armor of God. This indicates that these are not things that all Christians necessarily already possess. When Paul issues his command in Ephesians 6:17, "And take *the helmet of salvation*" (italics added for emphasis), Paul is writing to Christians (people who already have salvation), yet they have never truly grasped the hope of this salvation as a free gift God has given them. Fortunately, Paul makes his point about the "helmet of salvation" even more understandable when he warns the Thessalonians in 1 Thessalonians 5:8 that they (and you and I also) need to put on "as a helmet, the hope of salvation." I trust that this makes things a bit clearer. All Christians have salvation. But not all Christians have the *hope* that their salvation provides.

Hope?

Bear in mind, the reason for putting on the armor of God is so that you can stand firm and resist the schemes of the Devil. When Satan launches his offensives at you, his objective is to get you to waver, to lose faith, and to watch you collapse. His prime strategy (when he aims at your head) is to go for your thoughts, your mind, your ego, your over inflated view of your own intelligence and interpretation skills. He wants you to believe erroneously, to begin to doubt and question God, to be miserable in your circumstances, to question the purpose of your own existence, and in due course, to lose all hope.

Once Hope Is Forsaken

You should be aware there was a time when Paul was a prisoner of the Romans and was being transported to Rome on an Alexandrian sailing ship. Along the way, the ship and her crew encountered bad weather. Since the storm season comes during the start of wintertime in the Mediterranean, the ship's captain, after some debate, convinced the centurion in charge of the security detail to allow him to lay in a course toward a certain harbor on the Isle of Crete and once there to winter over. This turned out to be a dreadful decision. Once on the newly plotted course, a violent storm with treacherous winds arose, and the ship was battered about. Despite the crew dragging the boat's anchor, reinforcing the hull of the ship with cables, and maneuvering with their best seamanship, it was all too clear that they were in mortal danger of sinking. Acts 27:18–20 tells part of the story. The next day, as they were being brutally storm-tossed, they started jettisoning the cargo. On the third day, they even began tossing the ship's rigging overboard. Neither sun nor stars appeared for many days, and it was obvious that this was no small storm that was assailing them. From that point, the crew lost all hope of being saved. They felt completely abandoned. When these men lost their hope, their courage also swiftly departed, and they became dreadfully afraid. Can you understand why? Because in their minds, all hope (reasonable belief) of being saved had ceased to exist.

Christians can easily become filled with fear, discouragement, and despair when they are unable to maintain the hope of or belief in their salvation. This is why the Devil focuses his attack on your head. He tries to get you to doubt that God can really save you. He wants you to think God won't save you and doesn't really care about saving you. He tries to convince you that you are a worthless sinner and that you were never really saved in the first place. The only defense you can employ against this maneuver of Satan's is to keep your hope alive by taking advantage of the protection provided by putting on the "hope of the helmet of salvation" and to remember what you learned in chapter two. Remember Ephesians 2:8–9, "For by grace you have been saved through faith; and that not of yourselves, it is the gift of God; not as a result of works, so that no one may boast." Never forget it is God Who has done the work, not you. Do you have faith in Christ? Then you, too, are a recipient of the grace of God. Remember what it says in Romans 10:9, "If you confess with your mouth Jesus as Lord, and believe in your heart that God raised Him from the dead, you will be saved." So I implore you, press onward toward the battle as well-trained and confident soldiers, and do what Paul intended for you to do when he wrote in Titus 2:13, "Looking for the blessed hope and the appearing of the glory of our great God and Savior, Christ Jesus."

Selah (Ground your gear, take time to pause and reflect.)

You are nearly ready to graduate from your "basic training" assignment but first I need to finish with the final item of the full armor of God. In 2 Corinthians 6:7, Paul talked of having "the weapons of righteousness for the right hand and the left." In Paul's day, when a warrior had a weapon in each hand, it was typically a shield in one hand and a sword or spear in the other. Symbolically speaking, these are also representative of your weapons of righteousness, which are an integral and vital part of your spiritual 782 gear. They are used for both defensive and offensive purposes. We've spent a great deal of time learning to use our defensive armor. It is time now that we stop "lolly-gagging" about and learn about the only offensive piece of the full armor God provides you with: the Sword of the Spirit, which is the true Word of God. So hop to it, recruit, if you want to live forever, that is.

6:17b The Sword Is the Word of God

"…and *the sword of the Spirit*, which is the word of God." (Eph. 6:17b, italics added for emphasis)

There is not much interpretation needed here, for Paul describes precisely what the sword of the Spirit is in the same verse, Ephesians 6:17, "And the sword of the Spirit, which is the word of God." When God speaks, what He says should cut your heart and life like a sword. In Revelation 1:16, John saw and wrote this descriptive phrase of Jesus: "And out of His mouth came a sharp two-edged sword." The Word of God, just like a soldier's sword, can defend against the demonic blows of the army of darkness or be used to strike fear in their hearts, just like Jesus wielded the sword in the desert when tempted by Satan.

The End Product of the Sword

Your sword has two edges, just as it was described in Hebrews 4:12, "For the word of God is living and active and sharper than any two-edged sword, and piercing as far as the division of soul and spirit, of both joints and marrow, and able to judge the thoughts and intentions of the heart." The sword can penetrate or adjudicate, execute or cure, set free or obliterate. I can see you wondering, "How can one sword have two such radically different effects?"

There is a story in the third chapter of Judges where we read of the Moabites defeating Israel. Israel was forced to serve Moab's King Eglon for eighteen long years. At last, the people of Israel cried out to the Lord, and God raised up a man called Ehud to deliver them. Judges 3:16 states, "Ehud made himself a sword, which had two edges, a cubit in length, and he bound it on his right thigh under his cloak." Ehud, who was a left-handed man, hid the sword on his right side. The security guards who searched people coming in to see the king were not very thorough and routinely only patted down the left side of most people because that was usually where a soldier's sword and scabbard would be located. In this way Ehud was able to get past the king's security without any difficulty. When he told King Eglon he had brought a secret message, the king cleared everyone from the room, and in Judges 3:21 Ehud stretched out his left hand, took the sword from his right thigh, and thrust it into the king's belly. This two-edged sword ended the life of the King of Moab and at the same time delivered the nation of Israel. The same sword took the king's life while it gave new life to Israel.

The Word of God acts in the same way. It pierces the heart of those who choose to obey it, while it judges the lives and hearts of all who refuse to pay attention and conform to it. At the end of this age, when Jesus brings judgment to the world that has rejected the Word of God, the people who have yet to respond will be "killed with the sword which came from the mouth of Him who sat on the horse" (Rev. 19:21). I would rather the Word convict me now than eradicate me later. Does that make sense to you? Think about it this way, if I am wrong and live my life according to the Word of God, what harm is done? None. If I am right and you fail to heed the call and conform your life, what price will be required of you? According to Scripture, you'll pay the ultimate price of eternal damnation and separation from God.

Training to Use Your Sword

How, then, do you best wield this offensive weapon against your foes in spiritual combat? You must train to use it in the same manner Jesus did. I assure you there is no weapon more powerful than the spoken Word of God. If you look closely at the Scriptures, you will find you have been provided illustrations of how to wage spiritual warfare and how to engage your enemy in battle.

Right after Jesus' baptism, the Spirit led Him into the wilderness for a time of testing. After forty days and nights without food, the Devil approached and said to Him, "Why not just turn these stones into bread?" He answered and said, "It is written, 'MAN SHALL NOT LIVE ON BREAD ALONE, BUT ON EVERY WORD THAT PROCEEDS OUT OF THE MOUTH OF GOD.'" (Matt 4:4)…The Devil then led him to the pinnacle of the temple and said, "Throw Yourself down. The angels will catch You." But Jesus responded, in Matthew 4:7, "it is written, 'YOU SHALL NOT PUT THE LORD YOUR GOD TO THE TEST.'" Then, the Devil showed Him all the kingdoms of the world and said, in Matthew 4:9–11…"All these things I will give You, if You fall down and worship me." Then Jesus said to him, "Go, Satan! For it is written, 'YOU SHALL WORSHIP THE LORD YOUR GOD, AND SERVE HIM ONLY'" Then the Devil left Him; and behold, angels came and began to minister to Him I want you to pay meticulous attention to how Jesus used the Sword of the Spirit to wage spiritual combat. He says, "It is written." He didn't call on angels to capture the Devil. He didn't make a big production of praying in opposition to the Devil's spiritual antagonism. He merely quoted the Word of God. That alone was suitable for the situation. Folks, the only way you're going to win each battle you stumble upon is by getting a good grasp on and using the Word of God in a proficient manner. In 2 Samuel 23:10, you can read about one of David's mighty warriors named Eleazar who "arose and struck the Philistines until his hand was weary and clung to the sword, and the LORD brought about a great victory that day." You must always remember, no matter how weary you become, as long as your hands, mind, and life cling unyielding to the Sword of the Spirit, the Lord will give you the victory.

How to Ineffectively Use the Sword

I don't usually like to include negative instruction or reinforcement as part of my training procedures but I am going to make an exception in this case. Primarily because I need to make clear that nothing useful has ever been or ever will ever be accomplished by just waving your sword around. Warriors have a term for this, they call this type of thing "saber rattling," and saber rattling or posturing has never won a single battle. It has, in fact, throughout history often brought about exactly the opposite. Many battles have been started and lost by "saber rattling." You must realize that your swords are sharp and dangerous instruments, forged to inflict grievous bodily harm, and can unintentionally create dreadful damage when improperly or unwisely employed.

Paul reminded Timothy of that fact in 2 Timothy 2:15, when he was advised of his responsibility to be "accurately handling the Word of truth." When translated from the Greek, this phrase "accurately handling" means, "to cut straight." When you raise the Sword of the Spirit, you've got to cut straight and with a definite purpose or "target" in mind. Too many people are out there flailing their swords around without ever seeking the requisite training to acquire the appropriate skill. They miss their targets more often than they hit them because they misquote, misappropriate, and misuse the Word. These "tin soldiers" can frequently be found taking verses out of context and lambasting anyone within earshot without possessing any idea of what God really intended for that Scripture to convey. Accuracy is a prerequisite for any bearer of God's armor. You would also be wise to speak these things in a timely manner, as was indicated in Ephesians 4:29, "According to the need of the moment."

You should also consistently examine and verify your motivation. Why are you swinging your sword? Is it with intent to kill? If so, are you sure of your target and is there anyone else in the way? Don't ever forget Peter's experience in the Garden of Gethsemane. He was sleeping when he should have been praying. He wasn't physically or spiritually prepared for the difficulty he was about to encounter. When the soldiers grabbed Jesus to arrest Him, Peter drew his sword, and "struck the slave of the high priest and cut off his right ear. But Jesus answered and said, 'Stop! No more of this.' And He touched his ear and healed him" (Luke 22:50–51).

I have watched Christians eagerly but blindly wielding their sword with the intent to completely devastate and mutilate, while having no earthly idea of what their intended target really is. Even in mortal combat I have seen inexperienced soldiers "rock and roll," as we combat veterans like to say, on full automatic, accomplishing little more than to give away their position and draw the concentrated fire of the enemy. So before you decide you are ready to go into battle, glance back on how you have been commanded to act as a trained Christian soldier. First Corinthians 16:14 says, "Let all that you do be done in love." If you're guilty of using your sword blindly and with the vile intent only to kill, you will find yourself facing the same situation Peter found himself in and Jesus will again heal the wounded, and openly chastise you. So commit to memory the axiom requiring you to always check your motivation. Remember you are only a private, or maybe a captain in Christ's Army, not its commander. Before I move along I want to teach you an axiom regarding the appropriate use of your weapon. It is a little saying I have lived by since I first put on a uniform and picked up a firearm at seventeen years of age. It goes like this, "Draw not without reason, and sheath not without honor."

How Much Training?

I have spent many, many hours training with the weapons of warfare that I have used in both my military and law enforcement professions. My life often depended on my expertise. However before I ever placed, as we modern centurions say, "one round down range," I spent many, many days just learning how to hold my rifle, revolver, or pistol in various positions. To grasp the sword you will be using in your spiritual combat correctly and use it in a correct and effective manner will require you to spend a great deal of time practicing with it. It takes all the fingers, the thumb, and palm of my hand to hold the firearm I carried as a police officer for more than thirty-four years. I was trained well with this weapon, and during my career I was considered a "Distinguished Expert." It is that same hand that has been required to wield my sword of truth just as accurately and efficiently.

Let's take a look at one method of grasping the sword, which concentrates on applying the grip properly. I need to thank Pastor Rick Warren of Saddleback Community Church in California for introducing me to this idea. It involves the hearing, reading, studying, memorizing, meditating, and applying of the Word to your life. If you count the things you need to do to hold your sword properly, you'll find you can write one of them on each digit of your hand and still have one to write on your palm. So let me teach you one way to really understand what it truly means to "get a grip" on your sword. On your little finger, write the word "hear." On your "ring" finger, write the word "read." On your middle finger, write the word "study." On your index or "pointer" finger, write the word "memorize." On your thumb write the word "meditate." Now, down in the middle of your palm write the word "apply." OK, try to grasp your Bible with any combination of individual fingers but not by using all your fingers and your palm at one time. How well do you think you could wield your sword using that technique? Not very well at all. But now that you have been exposed to the things it really takes to get a grip on your weapon, you will find it will be much easier and you'll become so familiar with it. It will become an integral part of your spiritual armor.

You may be asking why it is necessary to do all of these things in order to become well trained in the use of the Word of God. OK, I'll let you in on a little secret: God said to do it! I could give you plenty of Scriptures to support that, and I guess I will. First I want you to realize you must grow as a Christian in order to wisely use the weapons of a mature Christian.

God tells us in Ephesians 4:14–15, We are not meant to remain as children but to grow up in every way into Christ." That is not an automatic process. You can see that by reading Hebrews 5:12–13, "You have been Christians for a long time now, and you ought to be teaching others, but instead you need someone to teach you. When a person is still living on milk, it shows he isn't very far along in the Christian life. He's still a baby Christian. Next you must realize that mastering the sword will take discipline. This is emphasized in 1 Timothy 4:7, where we learn we must "take the time and the trouble to keep yourself spiritually fit." Now let's look at just what God says about each of the elements of grasping the sword. We will see if God has anything to say about hearing. Do you think he does?

How about starting with Romans 10:17: "Faith comes from hearing the Word of God." And Jesus also said, "He who has ears to hear, let him hear!" Don't forget James 1:19, which says, "Be quick to listen." And Hebrews 2:1 points out "we must pay more careful attention to what we've heard, so that we do not drift away!" There is a problem with just listening, though. The problem is we tend to forget 95 percent of what we hear within seventy-two hours. So God reminds us that listening is not enough. In James 1:22 He says, "Do not merely listen to the Word and so deceive yourselves. Do what it says."

Next we need to look at what he says about reading, so let's start with Revelation 1:3: "Happy is the one who reads this book and obeys what is written in it." And then look at Deuteronomy 17:19: "The Scriptures shall be his constant companion. He must read from it everyday of his life so that he will learn to respect the Lord, his God, by obeying all of his commands" (LB) OK, now it is time to see what He says about studying. In Acts 17:11 He says, "They accepted the message eagerly and studied the Scripture every day." And don't forget, 2 Timothy 2:15 tells us we are to be good workmen.

Then we move on to memorizing. Just look at this list: Proverbs 7:2–3 says, "Guard my words as your most precious possession. Write them down, and also keep them within your heart." Or Psalm 119, where it says, "I have hidden your Word in my heart that I might not sin against you...Your Word is a lamp to guide me and a light for my path...Your promises to me are my hope. They give me strength in all my troubles. How they refresh and revive me." Proverbs 22:18 says, "You will be glad if you remember them and you can quote them." Then there is Jeremiah 15:16, "Your words sustain me. They bring joy to my sorrowing heart and delight me" (Living Bible). Now look at 1 Peter 3:15, "Always be prepared to give an answer to everyone who asks you to give the reason for the hope that you have."

Now on to the last finger: meditate. Look at all God has to say about this in Proverbs 4:23, "Your life is shaped by your thoughts." Romans 12:2 says, "Be transformed by the renewing of your mind." And again in 1 Corinthians 3:18 it says, "As we contemplate the Lord's glory, we are being transformed into His likeness." John 15:7 tells us, "If you live your life in Me, and My words live in your hearts, you can ask for whatever you like, and it will come true for you." And finally, in Joshua 1:8 it says, "Meditate on the word day and night, so you may be careful to do everything written in it. Then you will be prosperous and successful."

Before we finish with the things God told us to do, we will have to take the training on using the sword of the Word of God one giant step further and apply it. Yes, God told you to do that too. Where? In James 1:22, where you are told, "Do not fool yourselves by just listening to the Word. Instead, put it into practice." And in Matthew 5:19, where He says, "Whoever practices and teaches these commands will be called great in the kingdom of heaven."

In conclusion, I hope you see just how critical it is that you train diligently to use the Word of God; do so skillfully, properly, and compassionately, all of which demand that you remain in a state of perpetual readiness. You need to become—if you are not already—involved in individual training and group training that has as its primary objective an emphasis on a great deal of practical application of the sword. Faithfully execute your daily devotions; include others in your Bible studies. Prepare for church services, and review the text and supporting verses afterward. As you acquire experience you will become fast and competent. You will know which verses to quote and when they are appropriate to use. When you take the time to consistently evaluate your motivation, you will seldom find it tainted. This simple technique of sword handling will ultimately lead to many offensive victories for Christ throughout your life. And you may even become "Master of the Sword" or a weapons instructor yourself.

Selah (Ground your gear, take time to pause and reflect.)

Well, while it may appear as though we have completed our study of the full armor of God, two important training points still face us that you must review thoroughly. In the last seven verses, Paul extends to the Ephesians some final encouragements on praying, reminds them of his state of affairs, and gives them a parting blessing. You will see that as he makes a seemingly simple statement about prayer, and you will be forced to study his words very circumspectly so that you as a full-fledged Christian combatant might apply them in the approved manner. Now while you're shining that armor and putting an edge on your sword, listen up!

6:18 Pray in the Spirit

"With all prayer and petition pray at all times in the Spirit, and with this in view, be on the alert with all perseverance and petition for all the saints..." (Eph. 6:18)

Just what does "praying in the Spirit" mean? There are almost as many ideas about what this means as there are Christians. I think it must have been fairly easy for the early Church to interpret, since Paul stated it so very matter-of-factly, as did Jude, when he wrote in Jude 1:20, "But you, beloved, building yourselves up on your most holy faith, praying in the Holy Spirit." It seems clear to me that Paul and Jude were both at ease using that expression without a lot of explanation. Conversely today, as so many people in the Church have meandered away from seriously studying the Bible and have become more obsessed with creeds and doctrines, a struggle has developed over the true meaning of these words. Those on the conservative side of the debate have a tendency to say, "'Praying in the Spirit' simply means praying in God's will." Those of the charismatic persuasion seem to stress, "No, 'Praying in the Spirit' means speaking in the heavenly tongues when you pray." OK, troops, if I left it up to you, would you pick this as your first major spiritual battle? Which of these interpretations is absolutely right? Or does either of them seem correct? Must I remind you that war is really over? Remember another lesson learned from Peter in the garden and choose your battles wisely; some are not worth fighting at all. This might just be one of those battles.

Tongues, Tongues, What Tongues?

This command to pray in tongues is a captivating but not unusual one. Reflect back on the fact that Paul himself said he prayed in tongues frequently. He told the Corinthians in 1 Corinthians 14:14, "For if I pray in a tongue, my spirit prays." Tongues are also described in the Bible as being spoken to God (1 Cor. 14:2), of His mighty deeds (Acts 2:11), exalting Him (Acts 10:45–46), giving thanks (1 Cor. 14:18), and blessing Him (1 Cor. 14:16). However, after some supplementary study, you will find that Paul is not speaking of praying in tongues when he exhorts the Ephesians to "pray in the Spirit." I believe this to be true because he tells them in Ephesians 6:18, "With all prayer and petition pray at all times in the Spirit." When you petition God, you are beseeching Him for the satisfaction of your needs. However, when someone prays in a tongue, they are not petitioning God, they are praising Him. Additionally, Paul tells them they should pray at all times in the Spirit. A fact which, if he were describing tongues, would apparently be in conflict with his declaration in 1 Corinthians 14:14–15, "For if I pray in a tongue, my spirit prays, but my mind is unfruitful. What is the outcome then? I will pray with the spirit and I will pray with the mind also." Another reason I have for feeling his reference to "praying in the Spirit" most likely does not refer to a heavenly language is that Paul has written this letter to all of the Christians in Ephesus, including wives, husbands, and children. His command was issued to all of them, and he does not qualify it with a "for those of you who have been granted this gift." You should remember Paul, in his writings to the Corinthians, told us that not every Christian speaks in tongues (1 Cor. 12:30; 14:5). "Ipso Facto," after perusing the content, the frequency, and the spectrum of Paul's proclamation, it appears clear to me and I hope to you that he is not at this juncture, exhorting the Ephesians to always pray in tongues.

What About the "In God's Will" Part?

Let us take a quick look before we examine the other side of this potential dis-agreement, the part that might indicate you are to pray in God's will. This seems to carry more weight regarding how you are to pray, with me anyway, especially when you read Romans 8:8–9, "Those who are in the flesh cannot please God. However, you are not in the flesh but in the Spirit, if indeed the Spirit of God dwells in you." Obviously, there is a difference between "in the Spirit" and "in the flesh" that should be clear by now to most of you. When you were in the flesh, you were constantly doing things your own way, follow-ing the commands of your own sinful nature. If you can't see anything else, you should see that Paul's objective here is to convey that you must never pray according to your own fleshly wishes, prejudices, or emotions, but with the leadership and direction of the Holy Spirit, who dwells within the heart of every born-again Christian soldier in the Lord's Legions.

Supernatural Leading

But does that mean you will never experience anything supernatural at all when praying in the Spirit? I wouldn't jump to that or any other conclusion too quickly. The meaning of this expression "in the Spirit" (pronounced in the Greek *"en Pnyoo-maen"*) throughout the Bible, can often be associated with having supernatural knowledge or revelation. One example I can think of occurred just after Jesus was born and is recorded in Luke 2:25–32:

> "And there was a man in Jerusalem whose name was Simeon; and this man was righteous and devout, looking for the consolation of Israel; and the Holy Spirit was upon him. And it had been revealed to him by the Holy Spirit that he would not see death before he had seen the Lord's Christ. And he came in the Spirit into the temple; and when the parents brought in the child Jesus, to carry out for Him the custom of the Law Simeon held the child and began to pray, Now Lord, You are releasing Your bond-servant to depart in peace, according to Your word; For my eyes have seen Your salva-tion, which You have prepared in the presence of all peoples, A LIGHT OF REVELATION TO THE GENTILES, and the glory of Your people Israel."

In the Spirit, Simeon was able to pray with supernatural knowledge. On another occasion years later, while Jesus was being questioned by the Pharisees, the following example was documented in Matthew 22:42–45:

"What do you think about the Christ, whose son is He?" They said to Him, "The son of David." He said to them, "Then how does David in the Spirit call Him 'Lord,' saying, 'THE LORD SAID TO MY LORD, 'SIT AT MY RIGHT HAND, UNTIL I PUT YOUR ENEMIES BENEATH YOUR FEET'"? If David then calls Him 'Lord,' how is He his son?"

David had correctly prophesied of the Lordship of Christ as he uttered these words "in the Spirit." Paul said earlier in your training that this mystery of Christ, explained in Ephesians 3:5, "has now been revealed to His holy apostles and prophets in the Spirit." Also noteworthy is the fact that, in the Spirit, John received many supernatural revelations. He saw a vision of Jesus (Rev. 1:10), was taken up into the throne room of God (Rev. 4:2), was carried away into a wilderness (Rev. 17:3), and saw the New Jerusalem (Rev. 21:10).

Thus, as you continue to study and grow in your knowledge of Christ and His Word and eventually learn to instruct others in the way to obey Paul's command to pray in the Spirit, you must be mindful that although this is not a direct command to speak in tongues, every time you pray, you must consistently rely on the supernatural leadership of the Holy Spirit. The Spirit should be in direct command of your life, to guide your prayers, and you must never resort to praying in the flesh.

Selah (Ground your gear, take time to pause and reflect.)

You have completed your basic training in the book of Ephesians, and now Paul is offering you three graduation gifts: an exhortation for prayer, his current résumé, and a peaceful benediction. So don't get anxious, soldier. As Yogi Berra puts it, "It ain't over 'til it's over."

6:19–20 Boldness and Persistence

"…and pray on my behalf, that utterance may be given to me in the opening of my mouth, to make known with boldness the mystery of

the gospel, for which I am an ambassador in chains; that in proclaiming it I may speak boldly, as I ought to speak." (Eph. 6:19–20)

I am hopeful that you have taken seriously and internalized the training you
have received and recall how Paul stated in verse 18 that the Ephesians should
be in prayer at all times for all the saints. Now Paul says, "Please, don't always
just pray for everyone generally, but pray for me specifically." He asks them to
pray that he continues to have the necessary physical and moral courage to
remain bold and continue to utter the Gospel of Christ at every opportunity.
That sounds like a really dedicated soldier to me.

Utterance, You Say, Why Not Eloquence?

He asked for prayer that "utterance" would be given to him in the opening of
his mouth. Paul knew, and you should also, that it was never his—nor is it
your—words that ever won anyone to Christ. It is only the Spirit of Christ
that wins people over to Christianity. So Paul asked for prayer, relying on the
fact that Jesus promised in Matthew 10:19–20, "Do not worry about how or
what you are to say; for it will be given you in that hour what you are to say.
For it is not you who speak, but it is the Spirit of your Father who speaks in
you." If you really want to wax eloquent, then give every utterance to the Lord.
When you become His instrument, what you say, sing, or even write will have
no earthly comparison.

Boldness, Not Arrogance

His second concern was that he would continue to speak boldly. Somewhere, I
heard a pastor relate the following about someone in a fellowship he once
shepherded, who said, "Frankly I can't believe Paul ever had a problem being
courageous or speaking boldly." Nevertheless, after many years of military
leadership, engaging in combat, teaching complex legal and administrative
matters, testifying in court, solving problems for folks during very chaotic
times, and having a reputation for saying it like it is, I can assure you that even
the most "in-your-face Drill Instructor" experiences times of intimidation and
fear. The simplest of circumstances can sometimes turn the most valiant of
men into a pile of pudding. I have shared the experience of combat and physical warfare with many of my fellow soldiers, sailors, and Marines, and I can
tell you with impunity, that every one of us experienced at least a modicum of
fear. The combatant who lacks fear lacks reason and is a danger to himself and

the well-being of those around him. The well-trained warrior learns to trust his training, his instructors, and his equipment and to control his fear and use it to his distinct advantage, while hoping against hope that his opponent can't match his training, dedication, and skill.

The courage to continue to do what is right in the adversarial face of what is popular, politically expedient, or results in personal gain or gratification is what is known as "Moral Courage." This moral courage is what allows you as a Christian soldier to experience fear, conquer it, control it, and retain your status as an effective part of God's Army. You will find that doing what is right and necessary in all circumstances (especially the difficult ones) will be quite satisfying. Still, I'm not asking you to enjoy the battles. No one detests combat more than the man who has commanded in battle, but no one is more prepared for engaging the enemy in the next battle than that same individual. Here is an example that I hope and pray will help you see what I mean. You remember the night Jesus was arrested and taken back into Jerusalem to the house of the high priest? Well, Peter trailed along behind the entourage all the way into the courtyard, and, while he was warming himself by the fire, a servant girl "drops a dime on him" and identifies him as having been with the Lord. This is documented in Mark 14:67–68, "And seeing Peter warming himself, she looked at him and said, 'You also were with Jesus the Nazarene.' But he denied it, saying, 'I neither know nor understand what you are talking about.'"

Remember, Peter was a big, strong man who a short time before was impetuously waving his sword, ready to do battle with anyone to protect His Lord; yet he was intimidated, not by a little slave girl but merely by what she said. I think that Peter was confronted by some of the same issues you and I face today.

Sometimes the fear of being publicly identified with Christ assails each of us. Some of you may be afraid of the idea that what you do or don't do while flying the colors of Christianity can and will be viewed by others as a reason or an excuse not to become a fellow Christian warrior. Paul's professed fear of public speaking is, I am told, far more common among teachers and preachers of the Gospel than you might imagine. Paul, by praying for this, clearly revealed that this was also an issue for him. Some of his difficulty on this battleground may have originated from the many times he preached the Gospel, only to be beaten and whipped for it (1 Cor. 11:23–27). It is entirely within reason that he'd begun to be troubled by hesitation. But Paul knew that boldness comes from the ministering of the Holy Spirit of God and not from within himself (2 Tim. 1:7; Acts 1, 4), so he wisely requested prayer.

Making the Mystery of the Gospel Known

Paul requested prayer for utterance and boldness so that he could continue to serve the Lord and make known the mystery of the Gospel. The Greek word for "mystery," as I am confident you will recall, is pronounced *"moos-TAY-ree-on,"* and is understood to mean, "something hidden, secret, unknown, or not obvious." Paul realized, and you and I must also, that many people in the world didn't and today still don't know the Gospel. It remains a mystery to them and will continue to until you or I, as Christian soldiers and ambassadors of Christ, unveil it to them. On more than one occasion, Our Lord and Savior issued the command that made it our sacred duty to bring them that message. He told the Romans, "How then will they call on Him in whom they have not believed? How will they believe in Him whom they have not heard? And how will they hear without a preacher?" (Rom. 10:14). Yes, my friend and fellow comrade-in-arms, Paul understood that this message was what he ought to speak, and he trusted God to know how he ought to speak it. It's just what he was supposed to do. He even told the Corinthians, "I am under compulsion; for woe is me if I do not preach the Gospel" (1 Cor. 9:16). Therefore, Paul asked the Ephesians to pray that he would be bold and not afraid to do what was required. Do I hear an amen chorus responding out there?

6:21–22 Sending Tychicus

> "But that you also may know about my circumstances, how I am doing, Tychicus, the beloved brother and faithful minister in the Lord, will make everything known to you. I have sent him to you for this very purpose, so that you may know about us, and that he may comfort your hearts." (Eph. 6:21–22)

Paul placed the Ephesians on the alert that Tychicus, pronounced *"Too-khee-KOS,"* would be coming to Ephesus. This individual labored frequently with Paul and shows up in Acts, Ephesians, Colossians, 2 Timothy, and Titus, yet not many people seem to remember him. I have even read somewhere along my sojourn that he was a pastor in the Ephesian Church. But, when you think about it, that anonymity is not all that bad. Shouldn't we all advocate the same low profile as we serve in Christ's Church? There are way too many people who are trying to make a big name for themselves or build themselves a reputation based on what they "allegedly" do for God instead of letting God work through them. I believe that some people are even scheming to become celebrities in the Kingdom. I would rather be invisible myself. I have learned that in combat, it is the sniper—a soldier who uses skill, silence, and camouflage—who strikes real fear in the hearts and minds of the enemy, one round at a time. It is my wish that any ministry of which I am a part will bear a lot of fruit, but that no one will necessarily remember my involvement before they remember the name of Jesus my Lord and my Life's Commanding Officer. I take to heart something a reverend said many years ago in a sermon. I am sorry I can't remember who said it, but it is written in one of my Bible margins. He said, "Don't ever let someone find your fingerprints on the ministry of Jesus." In light of this, I trust that Tychicus' reward will be greater than that of many men whose names are more recognizable.

Don't Worry about Me

Tychicus was dispatched for three reasons. His mission was to carry the message of Paul's circumstances, to tell the Ephesians about Paul's personal well-being, and to comfort their hearts. One very admirable quality Paul possessed was his perseverance. Paul wasn't a whiner. He was almost indifferent to his own uncomfortable circumstances. He was, however, consistently concerned with the state of the affairs of the people who might be worrying about him. That is why he frequently sent letters or messengers with inspirational words, like, "I'm doing fine. I'm OK. I'm rejoicing in the Lord." We as Christians today can learn a real lesson from how Paul filled this void in the lives of others. Have you noticed how Christians today tend to send word only when they're doing poorly? It seems the only time some of them even talk to God is when things in their lives are in chaos. I've noticed all too frequently that many people's prayer requests are always so frantic and filled with calamity. It would be nice once in a while just to hear an encouraging word being transmitted (on the commo net) up to Heaven, wouldn't it? "Yes, I'm in prison and being starved, but I'm holding onto my Lord and will take a rain check on giving up my hope in God." Even when Paul was in prison, seemingly abandoned, hurt, and betrayed by so many people, he wrote to Timothy about his circumstances, saying in 2 Timothy 4:17–18, "But the Lord stood with me and strengthened me." Yes, I'd love to receive the encouraging message that says, "I'm doing well. Definitely pray for me, but don't worry about me."

6:23–24 A Grace-filled Benediction

"Peace be to the brethren, and love with faith, from God the Father
and the Lord Jesus Christ. Grace be with all those who love our
Lord Jesus Christ with incorruptible love." (Eph. 6:23–24)

At long last, Paul speaks a final blessing to the Ephesians, reminding them
that peace, love, and faith all come through grace from God the Father and
the Lord Jesus Christ, and that this grace is available for all those who love
Jesus with a love that will never die or decay.

Well, Soldier, You Finally Made It to Graduation

Now, soldier, you have enough training to no longer be called a "boot," and it
is time for you to graduate from "Boot Camp." But you still need to realize you
are like most Christians, just a Private starting out in God's "Army of the
Saved." There are a few things I want to reiterate, before we part ways, about
things that are in your future. Some of these things are likely to be in your
immediate future! If you trained with any degree of seriousness, you will be
engaged in battle before you realize it. Satan doesn't waste his time doing battle with the uncommitted; they do not require his personal attention. When
he attacks you, it will be with a ferocity you may have never known. He will
use many of the methods we have discussed and may use some we have not
even considered.

You will require, just like any new Marine or Soldier, recently out of basic
training, some advanced training in tactics, continued weapons familiarization
and requalification, a growing understanding of enemy intelligence, and some
advanced individual combat techniques. I suggest you find a local church fellowship where you can get these skills and practice this advanced training. You
will also become much more secure in your faith if you pick up a "ranger
buddy" with whom you can partner up for advanced training (discipleship and
accountability). Individuals and small groups of fellow Christians will increase
your chances of survival as you learn to work together and provide the mutual
support you both will need. There truly is strength in numbers. You are now a
part of a "Band of Brothers," and you will need the sage advice of veteran
Christians. It will be of great assistance in learning to tell friend from foe and
right from wrong. You will need and want them to train side-by-side with you
as you learn to stand steadfastly in the gap. Never forget, soldier, the war is
really over, it ended with Christ's death and Resurrection at Calvary, but there

are still many deadly battles yet to be fought. So stand vigilantly, courageously, and responsibly as you endeavor to take your place on the front lines.

I leave you in good hands: God's hands. I also salute you and commend you until we serve together again.

I am praying about a sequel to this undertaking if My Lord so leads me. I'll write one based in Timothy this time, for it is in Timothy that the characteristics and leadership traits of the veteran Christian soldier are examined, evaluated, and preserved for eternity.

The Marine Corps taught me to serve well My God, My Country, and My Corps!

Semper Fidelis
(Always Faithful)
The Fairman Family Motto
Firmus en Christo
(Steadfast in Christ)
TEN-Hut!
Dismissed!

978-0-595-36445-9
0-595-36445-4

Printed in the United States
44595LVS00004B/199-285